Aristotle
On Poetics

Translated by Seth Benardete and Michael Davis

With an introduction by Michael Davis

St. Augustine's Press
South Bend, Indiana

Manufactured in the United States of America.

2 3 4 5 6   23 22 21 20 19 18 17 16

Library of Congress Cataloging in Publication Data
Aristotle.
   [Poetics. English]
   Aristotle's On poetics / translated by Seth Benardete and
   Michael Davis with an introduction by Michael Davis.
      p. cm.
   Includes index.
   ISBN 1-58731-025-2 (hardcover : alk. paper)
   ISBN 1-58731-026-0 (pbk. : alk. paper)
   1. Poetry – Early works to 1800. 2. Aesthetics – Early
   works to 1800. I. Title: On poetics. II. Benardete, Seth.
   III. Davis, Michael, 1947- IV. Title.
PN1040.A513 2001
808.2 – dc21   2001005879

∞ The paper used in this publication meets the minimum requirements
of the American National Standard for Information Sciences Permanence
of Paper for Printed Materials, ANSI Z39.481984.

ST. AUGUSTINE'S PRESS
www.staugustine.net

Aristotle – On Poetics

Contents

Preface

Aristotle's *On Poetics* has been widely read, and deservedly so, simply as a treatise on tragedy. It is telling that the book that provides a historical account of the development of tragedy as the perfection of poetry and yet praises the oldest of the poets as the best of the poets should at once stand at the beginning of the history of literary criticism and be the greatest work in the tradition it inaugurates. Since, as one might expect, there have been countless translations of *On Poetics*, one might legitimately wonder what justifies yet another. We began this translation with the intention of providing a useful complement to *The Poetry of Philosophy: On Aristotle's* Poetics, the argument of which is meant to establish that *On Poetics*, while certainly about tragedy, has a concern that extends beyond poetry to the very structure of the human soul in its relation to what is.[1] Since this is not immediately apparent, excavating the argument of *On Poetics* proves to require attending not only to what is said on the surface but also to the various puzzles, questions, and peculiarities that emerge only on the level of how Aristotle says what he says and thereby lead one to revise and deepen one's initial understanding of the intent of the argument. It is perhaps not altogether shocking that someone who devotes such attention to how tragedy ought to be composed should be concerned as well with the how of his own writing. With its issues framed in this way, *On Poetics* turns out to be a rather beautiful piece of literature in its own right.

[1] This is possible because in dealing with what cannot be otherwise, tragedy reflects the necessity of the impossible both in the stories it tells and in its manner of telling them.

Naturally how one understands Aristotle's manner of writing in *On Poetics* has consequences for how one will translate him. If the book is not properly speaking a writing at all but a collection of lecture notes the intention of which, while generally quite clear, is occasionally dark owing to Aristotle's infelicitous choice of words, then a translator will have as his task rendering the sense of what is obvious and striving to clarify what Aristotle has left obscure. If, on the other hand, *On Poetics* is an artful composition, a translator will seek to preserve interesting ambiguities, translate Greek terms consistently with a single word as much as is compatible with intelligible English so as to preserve allusions in the text that suggest otherwise odd but perhaps fruitful comparisons, and not change sentence structures gratuitously. Now, even if *On Poetics* were simply a collection of notes, as long as this sort of fastidiousness results in readable English, nothing would be sacrificed. And if *On Poetics* is something more than that, of course, a great deal would be gained from translating scrupulously. Accordingly it seems a wager in the spirit of Pascal to translate *On Poetics* as literally as possible, and we have endeavored to do so in this spirit.

The choice of crucial terms for a translation that strives to be literal is frequently difficult, and necessarily sometimes impossible. *Muthos* clearly means plot, and everyone translates it this way. However, before Aristotle appropriates it for *On Poetics* and uses it in a rather technical way to refer to the plot of a drama or of an epic poem, insofar as *muthos* refers to stories, they are always either about the gods or have in some way a divine origin. In no other work of Aristotle is *muthos* used to mean plot. His very special use of the word thus calls our attention to the marked absence of the question of the gods in *On Poetics*, an absence very peculiar given the role of the gods in the extant tragedies.[2] In appropriating for a

---

[2] No less peculiar is the suppression of the political as an issue. The word *polis* occurs only twice in *On Poetics* and in rather insignificant contexts.

rational account a term that ordinarily involves the divine, Aristotle cannot simply be denying the import of the gods for tragedy as it had existed historically. Is it possible, then, that he means to provide in *On Poetics* an account of the deeper function of which the presence of the gods in particular tragedies is merely the surface manifestation? That is, is Aristotle's long treatment of the centrality of plot for tragedy meant to be connected to the centrality of the sacred in human life as providing a limit beyond which one cannot go and remain human? We have chosen the less technical "story" as a translation of *muthos* and added a note explaining our choice in the hope of keeping open issues of this kind; after Aristotle "plot" falls perhaps too easily for us into the category of a part of fiction. In *On Poetics*, as in his other works, Aristotle frequently uses ordinary words in rather exotic ways, coins words, or resuscitates words dying out of the language. He is such a powerful thinker that we who come after him have tended to take these departures from the ordinary language for granted. To preserve Aristotle's original meaning it is sometimes necessary to avoid the technical vocabulary he originates (e.g., we have rendered *katharsis* as "cleansing") or to transliterate certain key terms (e.g., *poiêsis*) so as to avoid prematurely narrowing their meanings. Many of the notes to the text are for the purpose of elucidating ambiguities of this kind.

This edition of *On Poetics* differs from others as well in providing in the notes to the text and in the appendices translations of passages found elsewhere in Aristotle's works, as well as in those of other ancient authors that prove useful in thinking through the argument of *On Poetics* both in terms of its treatment of tragedy and in terms of its broader concerns. It is our hope that by following the connections Aristotle plots between *On Poetics* and his other works readers will begin to appreciate the centrality of this little book for his thought on the whole.

The text of Aristotle's *On Poetics* rests primarily on two Greek manuscripts and translations, one in Arabic and two in Latin.

Accordingly, the text is at times corrupt for several lines, and extensive interpolations have been suspected. Many scholars have contributed to the interpretation and/or correction of *On Poetics*. Besides the various editions of Butcher, Bywater, Else, Gudeman, Kassel, and Lucas, we wish to single out Johannes Vahlen's *Beiträge zu Aristoteles' Poetik* (Leipzig-Berlin 1914). We wish also to thank Ronna Burger for reading through the whole translation with care and for making numerous valuable suggestions for its improvement. An earlier version of this translation was used in Michael Davis's course on Greek Tragedy at Sarah Lawrence College; we thank his students for noticing errors and pointing out passages that were unnecessarily unclear.

     *   *   *   *   *

In the autumn of 2001, Seth Benardete took ill; he died on November 14. During the weeks before his death we worked together on the page proofs of the translation of *On Poetics* and made the few corrections that were necessary. At the time I did not know that this would be the final stage of an ongoing conversation that lasted for over twenty years. Benardete's mastery of Greek and Latin texts was legendary. He was, to be sure, a great scholar – perhaps the ablest classicist of his generation – but scholarship was never his primary concern. For Benardete, to read a book meant finally to look past it to the world it describes – to philosophize. Seth Benardete was an extraordinary man from whom it was my great privilege and delight to learn. His friendship was a gift beyond measure.

Introduction

Of Aristotle's writings none has had more staying power than *On Poetics*. It has been commented on by scholars too numerous to name and even more impressively by the likes of Averroes and Avicenna (even though they seem to have had at best a very unclear idea of what a tragedy was[1]), Racine and Corneille, Lessing and Goethe, Milton and Samuel Johnson.[2] Yet all this interest seems rather queer given the subject matter of the book. *On Poetics* is about tragedy.[3] But Greek tragedy is very unlike our drama. To

[1] Although they do not seem to have possessed any tragedies, their commentaries are filled with interesting remarks. Still, Aristotle's account alone was not enough for Avicenna to recognize that tragedy was more than "the praise meant for a living or dead person."

[2] See Averroes, *Averroes' Middle Commentary on Aristotle's* Poetics, C. Butterworth, trans. (South Bend, Ind.: St. Augustine's Press, 2000); Dahiyat, I.M., *Avicenna's Commentary on the Poetics of Aristotle: A Critical Study with an Annotated Translation* (Leyden: Brill, 1974); Corneille, Pierre, "Discours de la Tragédie" in *Théatre complet*, vol. 1 (Paris: Garnier, 1971), 33–56; Racine, Jean, Preface to *Phèdre*, (Paris: Larousse, 1965); Lessing, G.E., *Hamburgische Dramaturgie*, Nrs. 73–83 in *Werke*, vols. 6–7 (Leipzig: Bibliographische Institut, 1911); Goethe, Johann Wolfgang von, *Nachlese zu Aristotelische Poetik* in *Goethe the Critic*, introduction and notes by G.F. Semnos, revised and completed by C.V. Bock (Manchester: Manchester University Press, 1960), 60–63; Milton, John, Preface to *Samson Agonistes* in *Poetical Works* (New York: American News Company, no date); and Boswell, James, *Life of Samuel Johnson, LLD*. (Oxford: Clarendon Press, 1934).

[3] The general, but not universal, view is that there were originally two books to *On Poetics*, one on tragedy and a second on comedy. In our text, recovered about 1500, there is no account of comedy.

mention only a few of its exotic characteristics, it is performed by at most three actors playing multiple roles, wearing masks, accompanied by a chorus that is both a character in the play and a spectator of it, alternating between song and dialogue, before audiences of up to 30,000 people. The chorus sings using one dialect and speaks in another. The very complicated poetic meter is based not on stress but on the length of syllables. Since the language was accented tonally, one would think singing in Greek would be particularly difficult to understand. How were the tones of the individual words combined with the tones of the tunes? So by our standards it was strange. But did it not endure for a long time? Not really – the great age of Greek tragedy lasts for less than one hundred years. In this it seems much less impressive than the novel. Greek tragedy pretty much spans the life of one man – Sophocles (and, curiously enough, also the life of Athenian democracy). But was it not at least very widespread? Again, not really – it was imitated of course, but tragedy is predominantly an Athenian phenomenon, restricted in large measure to the area of Greece called Attica – hence Attic tragedy. All of the Greek plays we now possess were originally performed in one theater – the theater of Dionysus on the slope of the Acropolis. Why then should we be concerned with a book written 2400 years ago about a literary form practiced for only a hundred years in a single theater in a city more or less the size of Peoria? That *On Poetics* is traditionally taken to be an important book, then, may be taken for granted; why this should be the case, however, is not so clear.

The first words, and traditional title, of the *On Poetics* are *peri poiêtikês* – on the art of whatever it is that the verb *poiein* means. Ordinarily *poiein* would mean "to do," especially in the sense of "to make." It is the French *faire* or the German *machen*. Then it gets a narrower meaning as well – to make poetry. So *peri poiêtikês* means "on the art of poetry." Aristotle will argue that tragedy is paradigmatic for poetry, and so the book about poetry can be primarily about its most perfect manifestation. At the same time there is considerably more at stake. At the end of his discussion of the historical origins of comedy and tragedy, Aristotle remarks that the Dorians lay claim (*antipoiountai*) to both, citing their names as signs.

> And they say they name doing [*poiein*] *dran*, but that
> the Athenians name it *prattein*. (1448b1–2)

While this seems scarcely more than a footnote, in the context of *On Poetics* Aristotle has invited us to consider *poiein* and *prattein* synonyms. Should we accept his invitation we would have to retranslate the title of Aristotle's most frequently read little book. *Peri Poiêtikês* would mean *On the Art of Action*. Actors and acting would have something to do with action; poetry would somehow be at the center of human life.

Circumstantial evidence favors such a view of *On Poetics*. If all human action seems to aim at some good, and if the existence of instrumental goods points toward a good for the sake of which we choose all the others, and if there is a science of this highest good, and if as Aristotle says this is political science, or *politikê* (*Nicomachean Ethics* 1094a), then one would expect *poiêtikê* and *politikê* to be very closely linked. They are. Aristotle's *Politics* ends with an account of music, and especially poetry, as both the means for educating men to be good citizens and the goal for which they are educated.

What all of this might mean becomes somewhat clearer in Aristotle's *Nicomachean Ethics*. In Book 3, courage or manliness (*andreia*) is said to be the proper mean with regard to the passions fear and confidence. However since fear can be understood as an anticipation (a *prosdokia* or foreseeing) of bad things generally, lest courage be thought somehow equivalent to all of virtue, the particular fear with which it deals must be specified. As the most terrible fear is of death, this must be what concerns courage – but not all death. Courage comes into play where it is possible for us to exercise choice. It is therefore most of all concerned with facing death in war.

To make this point Aristotle compares drowning at sea with fighting a battle. The comparison recalls *Iliad* Book 21 where Achilles fights with a river – called Xanthus by the gods and by us, and Scamander by Achilles and the Trojans. Achilles laments the possibility that he might die in this ignominious way; to us who are aware that he is fighting with a god, his fate does not look so disgraceful. Aristotle knows, of course, that it is possible to be courageous in a hurricane, but thinks such courage is understood metaphorically. The paradigm is always fighting in battle. The account of the specific moral virtues, therefore, begins with courage because courage is a model for how to deal with all fear understood as *prosdokia* of the bad, and so for how to deal with the bad generally. Aristotle focuses on a situation in which we have a choice so as to provide a model for behaving always as though we had a choice. Accordingly, Achilles is not simply the most courageous but the model for virtue altogether.

The hardest problem for Aristotle's account of courage is that, while the moral virtues are supposed to make us happy, courage is frequently rather unpleasant and can easily make us dead. In fact the virtue one usually thinks of as attached to deeds of daring has nothing to do with skill in killing and is almost exclusively concerned with the appropriate attitude toward dying. Why, then, does the brave man risk his life? Aristotle says it is for the sake of the *kalon* – the noble or beautiful. But this *kalon* end is clearly not present in the activity itself. Neither killing nor being killed is by itself beautiful. We must look beyond the dead bodies fouling the Scamander to see Achilles' devotion to the *kalon*. The brave man, presenting an image to himself of his action as completed, looks at his deed as others will look at it, and so reaps the benefits of honor even before it has been granted. The present action becomes *kalon* insofar as it is made complete through reflection or imagination. The brave, therefore, do what they do not because it is good, but because they can say "it is good." This is what the *kalon* means.

The highest of the spurious forms of courage is political courage; its goal is honor. For examples Aristotle quotes Hector and Diomedes worrying about what will be said of them if they do not fight. But just what is it that differentiates this from acting "for the sake of the *kalon*?" If courage always means courage in war, then it will always manifest itself in a political context. Cities make war; individual men do not. But if courage is a virtue, it ought to be something that transcends any particular *polis*. This is just the problem of Achilles. Apart from the *polis* he cannot show his virtue, but once he returns to the fighting his motives are necessarily obscure. Does he return for the sake of Patroklos, of the Greeks, of honor, of immortality? *Andreia* is in principle invisible, for one cannot see it apart from a political context, which is to say apart from the ulterior motives for action that are attributed to the political man.

The most startling thing about the account of courage in the *Nicomachean Ethics* is that Aristotle uses almost exclusively fictional examples – Achilles, Hector, Diomedes, etc. Without poetry there is virtually no possibility of seeing that element that makes courage what it is. The brave man does not risk his life out of a greater fear, or shame, or confidence owing to superior experience. And yet from the act itself it is impossible to tell the difference between these spurious forms of courage and the real thing. We need the whole story, and only poetry gives it to us. Poetry lets us see inside men so that we can celebrate their devotion to the *kalon*. This points us back to the earlier account of the metaphorical character of courage in a storm at sea. In a way, *all* courage is metaphorical. Even Achilles is playing a role; he knows his fate, and is therefore the paradigm of the courageous man; like all brave men, he wants "to die like Achilles." Poetry makes it possible to experience our action as whole before it is whole. This wholeness then becomes a part of the experience itself. Or rather, since the conjunction does

Introduction

not really occur temporally, poetry constitutes the experience. In the case of courage, what would be essentially painful is transformed into something "pleasant."[4] And insofar as courage represents all moral virtue here, poetry would be the necessary condition for moral virtue generally. That we can contemplate the possibility of our own deaths is what makes it possible for us to attempt to fashion our lives as wholes, but as we never really experience our lives as wholes, this contemplation is a sort of fiction. It is poetic.

One can go one step further. Aristotle begins *On Poetics* by addressing two apparently different issues – the *eidê* of poetry and their powers and how to put a poem together out of its parts. Aristotle begins *On Poetics* in the following way:

> Concerning poetics, both itself and its kinds [*eidê*], what particular power each has, and how stories [*muthoi*] should be put together if the *poiêsis* [poetry, making, thing made] is to be beautiful, and further from how many and from what sort of proper parts it is, and likewise also concerning whatever else belongs to the same inquiry, let us speak, beginning according to nature first from the first things. Now epic poetry [*epopoiia*] and the making [*poiêsis*] of tragedy, and further comedy and the art of making dithyrambs [*dithurambopoiêtikê*], and most of the art of the flute and of the cithara are all in general imitations.

Aristotle is conducting a class at once in fiction writing and in literary criticism; his subject, *poiêsis*, is both the making and the thing made. An account of the art of making involves an analysis – a taking apart – of how things are put together (of course the pieces out of which something is put together are not necessarily the same as the pieces of our understanding of how it is put together).

---

[4] See *On Poetics* 1448b10–20.

Directly after the methodological remark in which he announces his intention to begin from the first things, Aristotle lists various forms of imitation. Presumably imitations are the first things from which Aristotle will make his beginning. But as always derivative from what they imitate, they are queer beginning points. For poetry the first things apparently are second things.

Insofar as all human action is always already an imitation of action, it is in its very nature poetic. This places the beginning of Aristotle's famous definition of tragedy – that tragedy is an imitation of action – in a new light.[5] *On Poetics* is about two things: *poiêsis* understood as poetry, or imitation of action, and *poiêsis* understood as action, which is also imitation of action. It is the distinctive feature of human action, that whenever we choose what to do, we imagine an action for ourselves as though we were inspecting it from the outside. Intentions are nothing more than imagined actions, internalizings of the external. All action is therefore imitation of action; it is poetic.

However plausible this connection between poetry and action, it does seem funny for tragedy to serve as the model for all human action. A full account of what we are to make of the turn to tragedy would require an interpretation of the whole of *On Poetics*.[6] Fortunately there is a shortcut which hints at what is at stake. The two meanings of *poiêsis* – doing and poetry – are related much as talking and singing, walking and dancing, acting and acting. Human doing is double; to overstate the matter, it has a self-conscious part and an unself-conscious part. We are rational animals. Poetry, connected to the self-conscious character of action, at the same time manifests the doubleness of human action within itself. Aristotle turns to drama because, to a degree even greater than narrative

---

[5]   See *On Poetics* 1449b24–28.

[6]   I have attempted an interpretation of this kind in *The Poetry of Philosophy: On Aristotle's* Poetics (South Bend, Indiana: St. Augustine's Press, 1999).

poetry, it reflects the distinction between doing and looking at doing – between acting and reflecting. On the one hand drama must attempt to convince its audience of the reality of its action; on the other hand it must always remain acting – actors always imply spectators. Or, as George Burns once said "The most important thing about acting is honesty; if you can fake that you've got it made." Tragedy is the highest form of poetry because it most embodies this doubleness. Now "story is the first principle and like the soul of tragedy" (1450a38–39);[7] the two principles governing it – the likely and the necessary – point back to the distinction between the perspective of the actor and that of the spectator. An action within a play must seem to have consequences which are likely to the character doing them and necessary to the spectator watching them. By virtue of its structure, a tragic story accentuates the tension between spectator and actor. The best tragedies involve

[7]   In *On Poetics*, as in Greek tragedy itself, the relation between story and character is deeply puzzling. Just as we do not, and are not at first meant to, understand why the Oedipus who is a wise and good king, even if he has a tendency to anger quickly, should be the man who kills his father and sleeps with his mother, we do not understand why for Aristotle story so far exceeds character in importance among the parts of tragedy. A full account of this excess would be a long story – perhaps the story of *On Poetics* as a whole. Suffice it to say here that character stands to story as the two parts of *mimêsis* – emulation and representation – stand to one another. Tragedy makes character, otherwise invisible, show itself externally; a story reveals a soul to us in such a way as to allow us to be able to say, "That's him!" That there is something artificial about the total agreement of story and character is clear from the *Nicomachean Ethics*, where the reverse movement must occur. We act for the sake of the good, the final good being happiness. But happiness requires that we take into account the story of our lives as wholes, something we are able to do neither while we live nor should there be a life after death. Accordingly, character substitutes for this inability to grasp our lives as wholes. The substitution, however, is not altogether effective since human happiness is not assured by being virtuous but depends as well on chance.

what Aristotle calls reversal (*peripateia*) and recognition (*anagnôrisis*). They are so to speak the soul of story. Now, if poetry is paradigmatic for action, and drama for poetry[8] – and if tragedy is the most complete form of drama, story the soul of tragedy, and reversal and recognition the core of a story – then by looking at Aristotle's treatment of recognition and reversal, we ought to be able to learn something about why tragedy is singled out as the model for human action.

Reversal is defined in Chapter 11 of *On Poetics*.

> What has been spoken of as change into the contrary of the things being done is reversal and this too, just as we say, according to the likely or necessary. (1452a22–24)

Aristotle's example is from *Oedipus Tyrannus*. A messenger has just come from Corinth with the "good news" that the king, Polybus, whom Oedipus believes to be his father, has died. Oedipus expresses some doubts about returning as the oracle had also concerned his relations with his mother, and Merope, Polybus's wife, is still alive. This messenger, never given a name (or in Greek even a pronoun) by Aristotle,

> on his coming, in supposing that he was going to cheer Oedipus and release him from the fear regarding

---

[8] That drama, as imitation of action, is the paradigm for all poetry is evident if one begins with Hesiod's claim that we know the muses "speak many lies like the truth" (*Theogony* 27). By presenting an alternative to the real as real, all poetry in saying what is not true has as its nature to conceal the true nature of the poet who created it. Drama, then, by making the poet invisible in its imitation of action is in a way poetry at its most pure. This vanishing from view of the poet goes together with the necessity that there be a viewing of action. See 1449b31: "Since they do [*poiountai*] the imitation by acting [*prattontes*], the ordered arrangement of the *opsis* [seeing, spectacle] would in the first place be of necessity some proper part of tragedy."

> his mother, once he had made it clear who he was, he
> did [*epoiêsen*] the contrary. (1452a25–26)

The "he" is ambiguous here. It could apply to Oedipus, and it could apply to the messenger. But as disclosing Oedipus' identity proves to require disclosing the messenger's identity, the ambiguity seems to make no difference. In either case the good news proves bad. Intending to free Oedipus from the fear of parricide and incest, the messenger reveals that it was he who had brought the baby Oedipus to Polybus and Merope. The result is "a change into the contrary."

Now, it is clear that reversal involves some violation of expectation. But whose? Since the reversal need not coincide with any recognition within the play, the expectations cannot be those of characters in the play. The *Oedipus* would not be dramatically affected were the messenger to leave before he discovered that his good news backfired. At the same time, since the turn of events involves not so much a change as a reinterpretation of what has already occurred, *some* recognition seems necessary. Reversal must, therefore, be *our* recognition as an audience that what we thought to be is not what we thought it to be.

The account of recognition begins with a reference to its etymology:

> Recognition [*anagnôrisis*], on the other hand, just as
> the name signifies, is a change from ignorance
> [*agnoia*] to knowledge [*gnôsis*], whether toward friend-
> ship or enmity of those whose relation to good or ill
> fortune has already been defined. (1152a29–32)

Recognition as an-agnorisis, is a privation of ignorance. But might we not understand its etymology as ana-gnorisis – knowing back or re-cognizing? As the very same syllables give us two quite different etymologies, it is not so obvious what "the name signifies." When this sort of ambiguity arises within a play, the conditions are present for recognition.⁹ A prior confusion is discovered in a way that alters the action of the play. Recognition is thus the awareness within the play, i.e., of a character, which parallels the audience's awareness of a reversal.

Recognition is most beautiful when it coincides with reversal – when the discovery within the play comes to be together with the discovery outside the play.¹⁰ Aristotle alludes to the recognition "most characteristic of story and most characteristic of action" as "the one previously mentioned" but more literally as "the one having been said" (1452a36–38). Now, presumably this means the most beautiful kind, i.e., where recognition and reversal coincide. At the same time, certain recognitions occur when a character comes to understand the significance of things that *he* has previously said. Oedipus does this sort of thing all the time. He promises to pursue the murderer of Laius as though Laius were his father (264–266). And he begins *Oedipus Tyrannus* by addressing those assembled around him as *tekna Kadmou* – children of Cadmus. Oedipus treats them as though they were *his* children; he does not realize that he too is a child of Cadmus, that those who, under his care as king, may be like children are also his brothers and sisters, his fellow citizens. For Oedipus, really recognizing who he is would involve discovering the significance of "what has been said." The beauty of Aristotle's claim that the best recognition is "the one having been said" is that it is an example of itself.

A plot in which events simply followed one another predictably, i.e., in which the likely turned out to be the necessary, in which, for

---

⁹ Consider Heracles' reinterpretation of the meaning of Zeus's promise that he would not die at the hands of anything living (*Trachiniae* 1157–78) – he first takes it to mean he will not die, but later understands it to mean he will be killed by the poison from the blood of the dead centaur Nessus.

¹⁰ It is worth noting that Aristotle does not say that the discovery is the same discovery.

example, an army of superior strength attacked an enemy and won, would contain *pathos* (suffering or undergoing) but not reversal or recognition. Reversal makes an audience reflect on the necessity of action that at first seems unlikely, for example, that Deianira's attempt to make Herakles love her should end by killing him. Recognition introduces inference into the play so that reflection on the likelihood and necessity of the action becomes a part of the action and so has further consequences within the play itself. The turning point in *Oedipus Tyrannus* is Oedipus' discovery of who he is.[11] This sort of action in which coming to knowledge is decisive is, not surprisingly, especially revealing of the rational animal.

If a story requires a change of fortune, and the best change involves the coincidence of reversal and recognition, in which direction ought the change to occur? It would be *miaron* – polluted or disgusting – were a man who is *epieikês* (sound) to move from good to bad fortune. In *Nicomachean Ethics* Book 5, Aristotle gives an account of *epieikeia* as a virtue more just than justice because correcting the necessary imprecision of law as general. The *eipeikês* characteristically demands less than his share because he recognizes that justice does not prevail in the world. *Epieikeia* is therefore morality which is at the same time critical of moral idealism.[12] To show a man with such moderate expectations moving from good to ill fortune would be shocking. On the other hand, to show the wicked moving from bad to good fortune would arouse neither pity nor fear but righteous indignation. Tragedy is apparently not meant

---

11   It is surely no accident that the "moment" at which Oedipus learns "who he is" should be so fuzzy. Directly after the messenger tells him he is not the son of Polybus, Oedipus seems as concerned that Jocasta will think him ill born as he is that he is really the son of Laius (1062–63).

12   See Burger, Ronna, "Ethical Reflection and Righteous Indignation: *Nemesis* in the *Nicomachean Ethics*," in *Essays in Ancient Greek Philosophy IV: Aristotle's* Ethics, edited by John Anton and Anthony Preus (Albany: SUNY Press, 1991), 130-34.

to cause utter despair of goodness in the world. Nor is it is especial-ly tragic to show the fortunes of the villainous change from good to bad. Such a plot might encourage *philanthropeia* – a sense of solidar-ity with other men – insofar as justice prevails, but it would result neither in pity (the villain gets what he deserves) nor in fear (the one who suffers is not like us). Tragedy, then, does not simply support morality and subverts moral naivete. Accordingly, Aristotle is silent about the plot in which the good man's fortune alters from ill to good. That tragedy is no simple morality play is signaled by a change in Aristotle's language. The "good" man – previously *spoudaios* or of stature (1448a2) – now becomes the *epieikês* – the sound man who is aware of the impossibility of perfect justice.

What remains then is what lies in between the *epieikês* and the bad man.

> He who is distinguished neither by virtue and justice nor changing to bad fortune on account of vice and wickedness is of this sort, but one who changes on account of some mistake and is one of those in great repute and of good fortune such as Oedipus, Thyestes, and notable men of families of this sort. (1453a7–12)

The subjects of tragedy are those who are thought to be great. Their repute (*doxa*) is a question of opinion (*doxa*). That their "mis-take" becomes a "great mistake" at 1453a16 has to do with the greatness of their repute in its connection to the rigidity of ordinary opinion. Their mistake has to do with being too little aware of the fuzziness of moral principles – too little *epieikês*. In one way such men are not virtuous; in another they are too virtuous.[13]

---

13   This is borne out by Aristotle's examples – Alcmeon and Orestes killed their mothers, but to avenge their fathers; Oedipus seeks to become mas-ter of his own fate, but to avoid the necessity to kill his father and marry his mother; Meleager is killed by his mother after accidentally killing his

According to Chapter 13 the change in plot must move from good to bad fortune. Curiously Aristotle seems to reverse himself in the following chapter. As actions may be done with or without knowledge, there are four possibilities for the action in tragedy. A character may intend to do something knowing what he is doing, but because of some accident not do it – this is not really drama. A character may intend to do something knowing what he is doing and do it – this is the case of Medea. A character may do something without intending to have done it and then discover what he has done – this is the case of Oedipus. Finally, a character may intend to do something, discover that he did not really know what he was doing and not do it – this is the case of Iphigeneia. Aristotle calls the last the best (1454a4). But how can it be best for Iphigeneia not to kill her brother, that is, for the play to have a happy ending, when tragedy requires a change from good to bad fortune?

Aristotle's language here is revealing. What the ancients did (*epoioun*) as well as what Euripides did (*epoiesen*) in the *Medea* was to make the doing (*praxai*) come to be with knowledge. Sophocles makes Oedipus do (*praxai*) terrible things in ignorance and then discover it. The "best" form is characterized as intending to do (*poiein*) and then, discovering, not to do (*poiesai*) it. Now, up to this point Aristotle had been using *poiein* to refer to the activity of the poet and *prattein* to apply to the activity of the character. Leaving this distinction intact, what is best would not be an action within the play but rather the action of the poet.

Let us see if we can pull some of the strands together. Reversal is an event in a play which leads the spectator to reflect on the events of the play. Recognition introduces this sort of reflection into the play as a piece of the action. By introducing the *epieikês*

uncles; Thyestes, brother of Atreus, seduced Atreus's wife, and, to punish him, Atreus feeds him his children; Telephon is punished for accidentally killing his uncles. These cases seem to point to conflicting moral issues which do not admit of straightforward solution.

Aristotle pointed to a kind of virtue, the highest kind, which is only possible as a reflection on the imperfection of virtue more conventionally understood. But why is this highest man not the subject of the highest form of poetic imitation? Poetry could never present the highest virtue if the highest, like *epieikeia*, necessarily takes the form of a reflection on the imperfection of the "best." No action could ever reveal the virtue which always takes the form of a reflection on action. Insofar as a poet wished to "present" the best he would have to present an action which causes reflection (i.e., reversal) rather than presenting the reflection itself (recognition). And insofar as human action approaches its best, the actor would have to present to himself an action which causes reflection. The activity of the *epieikês* is something like literary criticism; it consists in seeing where others have gone wrong.

Still, Aristotle certainly says that the best plot, and so the best tragedy, combines reversal and recognition – it makes reflection an action. Tragedy thus distinguishes itself from other forms of poetry by making the poetic character of human action thematic. However, to present in action a successful reflection on action (*epieikeia*) would not arouse wonder and so lead to reflection; it would be too pat, and so essentially invisible. The goal of tragedy is the stimulation of pity and fear because reflection is stimulated only by failure – "All happy families are alike; each unhappy family is unhappy in its own way." There is no wonder without some appearance of discrepancy. Therefore, the options for combining reversal and recognition seem to be these. The poet can either show the failure of genuine *epieikeia* which does not seem possible since *epieikeia* consists in the ability to foresee the ways in which one cannot expect virtue to be manifest in the world. How could a disposition the very nature of which is to be sound in its avoidance of excess be shown to be excessive? Or, the poet can show the failure of spurious reflection. This is in fact what occurs when reversal becomes recognition. Recognition will always in some sense be false recognition. It will therefore always be subject to a higher order reversal, and so it will stimulate wonder. Oedipus thinks that he knows who he is, but when he takes the pin of Jocasta's brooch, stabs himself in his eye sockets (*arthra*) and pleads to be set out on Mt. Cithaeron, he is simply reproducing what had been done to him as a baby when his joints (*arthra*) were pinned and he was abandoned on Mt. Cithaeron.[14] If he really knew "who he was" Oedipus would not once again be attempting to take his fate into his own hands. Blinding himself was not an altogether humble thing to do. He still has not learned that he too is one of the *tekna* of Cadmus. However, had he learned who he was, we would have been unable to learn who he was. Character, perhaps the true object of imitation in tragedy, is invisible except through plot.[15] For this reason, in his ranking of the various forms of recognition in Chapter 16, Aristotle finds particular fault with that sort which is willed by the poet. Where a character simply reveals who he is, the meaning of the recognition is altogether hidden from view.[16] The *epieikês* can express his knowledge even to himself only by articulating what would happen to him were he not to know. Oedipus could only have expressed wisdom by writing his own tragedy.

To be a rational animal does not mean what it seems to mean. It does not mean that there is a battle within us sometimes won by our good part and sometimes won by our bad part. This would make us monsters. The mixture is more intimate than that. As the tragic formula indicates, we learn through suffering or undergoing (*pathei mathos*); there is something irrational about our rationality.

---

[14] See Seth Benardete, *Sophocles' Oedipus Tyrannus*, in *Ancients and Moderns* (New York, 1964), pp. 1–15.

[15] Notice how the long-awaited discussion of character in Chapter 15 quickly gets derailed and turns into a discussion of plot. This movement perfectly mirrors the dependence of character on plot.

[16] On the importance of seeing for tragedy see Chapter 17.

Accordingly, Aristotle's examples of the best forms of recognition all involve a figuring out (*sullogismos*) which turns out to be a paralogism. Tragedy has as its goal making visible the most important thing about human beings, which, as essentially invisible, cannot be shown as it really is. The action which poetizes the world cannot be shown in poetry.

It is the story alone that differentiates one tragedy from another and what constitutes the story is *desis* (entanglement) and *lusis* (unraveling). *Desis* includes the action from the beginning or *archê* (which frequently includes events prior to the beginning of the play) up to the extreme point (*eschaton*) where the weaving together of the events of the story stops and things begin to unravel. The *lusis* is all the rest from the *archê* of the change until the end (*telos*) of the play. Now there is no question that in some sense Aristotle means us to take this account linearly or temporally. There is a part of any tragedy in which things are put together and a part in which they are taken apart. At the same time, the key terms of the account all allow for an alternative interpretation. Suppose *archê* means not temporal beginning but first principle, *telos* not temporal end but purpose, *eschaton* not temporal or spatial extreme but utmost, and, most important, *lusis* not denouement but resolution understood as something like ana-lysis. For this last there is evidence internal to *On Poetics* where Aristotle uses *lusis* to mean solution or resolution (1460b6, 1461b24) and *luein* to mean to solve or resolve (1460b22). *Lusis* appears, before having been defined, in Chapter 15 (1454a37) where Aristotle indicates that it ought to come out of the story itself and not be generated "from the machine." Now, if *lusis* meant analysis or interpretation here, Aristotle would be saying that tragedies ought to supply their own analyses.

This would explain Aristotle's emphasis in the sequel on the fact that poets are often quite good at *desis* (that is what it means to be a poet – to make up stories) but less frequently good at *lusis*. This is his version of what Socrates says of the poets (*Apology* 22c) – that "they say many beautiful things but know nothing of what they say." Poets, ordinarily good at the part of *poiêtikê* which involves putting the parts of a poem together, are not as a rule so good at the other part – analysis of poems according to their *eidê*. Tragedy is a crucial exception to this rule, for in tragedy part of the story is its *lusis*, an analysis of its action. Tragedy is distinct in being simultaneously synthetic or genetic – *desis* – and analytic or eidetic – *lusis*. On one level, then, the movement from *desis* to *lusis* is simply linear – there is a point in the play where things begin to unwind. On another level *desis* and *lusis* are the same. Once Oedipus utters his first words, *O tekna kadmou*, the meaning of his incest has already been revealed. Tragedy is something like a metaphorical analysis of metaphor in which events function simultaneously as parts of a play and *eidê* of its analysis. Things which look at first accidental in retrospect become absolutely necessary. *Lusis* in its deepest sense is not a part of the plot but a second sailing – a rereading which makes visible what was implicit from the outset but could never have been seen without first having been missed.

Tragedy is especially revealing of human action because it not only tells a story that is significant or meaningful, but also makes the fact that the story can be meaningful a part of the story it tells. *Pathei mathos*, the lesson of tragedy, is at the same time the structure both of human action and of human thought. *Human* action is imitation of action because thinking is always rethinking. Aristotle can define human beings as at once rational animals, political animals, and imitative animals because in the end the three are the same. In human action as in tragedy everything depends upon the intention of the actor. But that intention cannot be shown directly – it has to be revealed through action. When a poet tries to introduce intention directly it looks arbitrary and so is indistinguishable from chance. The true *deus ex machina* is therefore the human soul; it disappears as soon as one makes it visible. Ironically, the significance of our actions becomes visible only by reversing what we thought the significance to be. But that, of course, requires the initial assumption that one can see significance without reversal. You have to assume that you can see someone's character in order to see his action. This is what allows you to have your impression of the action reversed as the tragic story turns on itself so that you can "see" the character in question. We must assume Oedipus innocent in order to understand his true guilt. Blundering would seem to be the fundamental character of human action and thought.

If thought, and so human action, is essentially poetic in its need to put in place and time what cannot appear in place and time, does that mean it is essentially tragic? That is, if the recognition of tragedy is always spurious recognition, doesn't that mean we are essentially incapable of getting hold of ourselves? It does and it doesn't. Tragedy depicts tragic action, but it is not itself tragic, for if we recognize ourselves in the spurious character of Oedipus' recognition we are not simply in the position of Oedipus.

That Aristotle understands this to be true of tragedy is clear from the great compliment he pays it. *On Poetics* is a very playful book. In the middle of his discussion of tragic mistakes, Aristotle muses about whether those who criticize Euripides "make a mistake" (1453a8–23).[17] And in a remarkable *tour de finesse* he digresses abruptly in Chapter 12 to discuss the chorus; the digression proves to be an example of how the chorus works in tragedy. Having introduced reversal and recognition, Aristotle moves without explanation to a short chapter on the parts of tragedy. So out of place does chapter 12 seem that many editors have suggested moving it (beginning

---

[17]   In fact these men who make a mistake (*hamartanousin*) make the mistake that occurs within tragedy. They demand that justice prevail in the world. And if Euripides appears to be the "most tragic" of the poets, perhaps it is because he does what he ought to do even when the end does not follow from his plot. That is, Euripides' action in writing as he writes, his uniform adherence to a rule, has the makings of tragedy.

with Heinsius in the seventeenth century), and many others (e.g., Butcher and Else) do not accept it as genuine. The chapter is certainly queer; at first glance, its list of parts – prologue, episode, exode, parodos, stasimon, and commos – seems connected to nothing else in *On Poetics*. Upon reflection, however, one notices that each part is defined in terms of its relation to the chorus. Now the chorus has a funny function in tragedy. They are a character insofar as what they say grows out of the plot – to understand the famous stasimon in *Antigone* about man as the being most *deinos* of all (simultaneously most canny and uncanny), one must understand what they make this claim in response to. At the same time the chorus reflect *on* the action of the plot, and so talk directly to the audience. The role of the chorus therefore allows them to participate on the levels of both reversal and recognition. The chorus are then in a way the defining feature of tragedy – Nietzsche notwithstanding, the spectator within the drama. It is therefore especially meet that Aristotle should discuss the chorus in a "digression." Chapter 12 of the *Poetics* functions just like a stasimon; because it seems only marginally connected to what surrounds it, a choral ode looks like a reflection on what comes before and after. It is both still within the dramatic time of the play and at the same time atemporal. This "chorale ode" has as its content the centrality of the chorus for tragedy and so sheds light on what is at stake in the discussion of recognition and reversal that surrounds it.

In this and countless other ways *On Poetics* is a clever imitation of tragedy. Aristotle announced in his very first sentence that *poiêtikê* would involve putting together genetic and eidetic accounts. It is not surprising then that his book should admit of being read on two levels. It is about tragedy, but it is also about human action. The first is its *desis*, the latter its *lusis*. Their deep unity is the unity of the human soul.

On Poetics[1]

1.

Concerning poetics, both itself and its kinds,[2] what particular
power each has, and how stories should be put together if

[1]   "Poetics" translates *poiêtikê*; it is the art of *poiein*, which means
first to make or do and secondarily to make poetry. *Poiêsis*, the
product of *poiein*, frequently takes on the narrower meaning of
poetry. Articulating the full meaning of *poietikê* is the task that
Aristotle sets himself in the book that comes down to us in the
English tradition as *On Poetics*. Because of the weight of this tradition and the obvious concern of the book with poetry and
especially tragedy, we have retained this translation. However it
should be kept in mind that *poiein* is a very common verb in
Greek, and that in principle the art dealing with it could have as
much to do with making or action as with poetry in the narrower
sense. Where an ambiguity of meaning seems possibly inten-
tional, the Greek verb will be placed in brackets after the translation. Virtually every occurrence in the translation of any form
of the verb "to make" is a rendering of the Greek *poiein*, and all
appearances of English words cognate with "poet" are translations of words cognate with *poiein*. It is perhaps significant that
the only time *poiêtikê* is coupled with *technê* (art or craft) is at the
end (1460b14), for it is precisely there that Aristotle distinguishes *poiêtikê* from any other art. At 1447a19–20 Aristotle indicates
that imitation comes to be not only by art but also by habit.

[2]   The word is *eidos*. In Plato it is used for "form" or "idea."
Elsewhere in Aristotle it is used for "species," especially as
opposed to *genos*, genus. *Eidos* is regularly translated as "kind."
Where the context demands another translation, *eidos* follows in
parentheses. Its cognate and almost synonym, *idea*, will be translated as "form."

the *poiêsis*[3] is to be beautiful,[4] and further from how many 10
and from what sort of proper parts[5] it is, and likewise also
concerning whatever else belongs to the same inquiry, let us
speak, beginning first according to nature from the first
things. Now epic poetry[6] and the *poiêsis* of tragedy, and further comedy and the art of making dithyrambs,[7] and most
of the art of the flute and of the cithara are all in general 15
imitations.[8] But imitations differ from one another in three

3   The meaning of *poiêsis* ranges from "making" or "something
made" to "poetry." We have transliterated it to avoid prematurely narrowing this range. See footnote 1 above.

4   The Greek word here is *kalôs*. In its adjectival form, *kalon*, it
means both beautiful and noble. We will translate it by both;
sometimes together, sometimes, where the context demands, we
will choose one or the other. Wherever another word is translated by "noble," the Greek term will follow the translation in
brackets; "beautiful" will always translate *kalon*. The opposite of
kalon, *aischron*, means both shameful and ugly; it will be translated similarly either by the conjunction of the two terms or as context demands by one or the other. "Ugly" will always translate
aischron; wherever "shameful" translates another Greek word,
the original will follow in brackets. The adverb *aischrôs* will be
translated similarly.

5   *Morion* will be translated as "proper part." *Meros* will be translated as "part" although when "part" occurs in the translation it
need not mean that *meros* occurs in the Greek text. Aristotle discusses the difference between the two terms in *The Parts of
Animals*, which might be translated more accurately as *The
Proper Parts of Animals*.

6   The Greek *epopoiia* combines *epos*, epic, and a word cognate with
the verb *poiein*.

7   The Greek *dithurambopoiêtikê* once again combines the word for
dithyramb with a cognate of *poiein*.

8   "Imitation" translates *mimêsis*; "to imitate" translates the verb
mimeisthai. The entirety of *On Poetics* could be understood as an

ways, for they differ either by being imitations in different
things, of different things, or differently and not in the
same way. For just as some who make images imitate many
things by colors and figures (some through art and some   20
through habit) and others through the voice, so also in the
case of the arts mentioned, all make the imitation in rhythm
and speech[9] and harmony, but these either apart or mixed
together. For example, both the art of the flute and the art
of the cithara (and whatever others are of this sort with   25
respect to their power, such as the art of the pipes) use only
harmony and rhythm. But the art of dancers uses rhythm by
itself apart from harmony (for they too through the
rhythms of the shape of their movements imitate characters, sufferings,[10] and actions). On the other hand, the art
using bare speeches[11] alone and the one using meters,   1447b8
whether mixing them with one another or using some one
family of meters, are in fact until now nameless. For we
would not be able to give any name in common to the   10
mimes[12] of Sophron and Xenarchus and the Socratic

attempt to articulate the importance of *mimêsis* for understanding human nature. Of the approximately 115 occurrences of the
term in Aristotle, some 80 are in *On Poetics*. *Mimêsis*, *mimêma*,
and *mimeisthat* occur about 300 times in Plato.

9   *Logos* will ordinarily be rendered by "speech" and *legein* by "to
speak"; where it is necessary to translate them otherwise, the
transliterated Greek text will be supplied in brackets.

10   "Suffering" translates *pathos* throughout; however it has a range
of meaning from "experiencing" or "undergoing" to "suffering."

11   Bare, or *psiloi*, speeches are those that are unmetrical.

12   *Mimos*, while apparently restricted here to a specific type of
mimêsis, or imitation, would be the most obvious name for the
entire class. Sophron wrote male and female mimes.

speeches, any more than if someone should make the imitation through trimeters or elegiacs or any other meters of
that sort.[13] Human beings, however, in connecting the
making with the meter, do name some elegiac poets and
others epic poets, not addressing them as poets with regard   15
to the imitation, but with regard to the meter they have in
common; for even if they publish something in meter about
medicine or natural science, men are accustomed to call it
by its meter. But nothing is common to Homer and
Empedocles except the meter. Hence it is just to call the
one poet, but to call the other, rather than poet, one who
gives an account of nature.[14] And similarly, even if someone   20
should make an imitation by mixing together all the meters,
as Chaeremon made the *Centaur* a rhapsody mixed from all
meters, one would also have to address him as poet. Now,
concerning these things, then, let them have been distinguished in this way. For there are some which use all the   25
things mentioned – I mean [*legô*], for example, rhythm,
song, and meter – such as the *poiêsis* of dithyrambics and of
nomes[15] and both tragedy and comedy. But they differ
because some use all at the same time and others use them
part by part. Now, among the arts I say [*legô*] the differences in what they make the imitation are these.

2.   1448a

Since imitators imitate those acting, and since it is

13   Athenaeus alludes to this passage at 11.112 (505C): "Aristotle in
     his *About the Poets* writes as follows: 'Are we not to assert that the
     completely unmetrical mimes of Sophron are stories (*logoi*) and
     imitations, or those of Alexamenus the Tean written before the
     Socratic dialogues?'"

14   The Greek is *phusiologos*.

15   *Nomos* initially means "melody" and later comes to mean "song,"
     including both words and music. It also means law or custom.

necesary for them to be either of stature[16] or inferior[17]
(characters are pretty nearly always consequences of these
alone, for everyone differs in point of character by vice or
by virtue[18]), they imitate either those better than what is on
our level or worse or even the sort that are on our level, just   5
as painters do. For Polygnotos used to make images of the
better, while Pauson of the worse, and Dionysius of the
similar.[19] And it is also clear that each of the aforesaid imitations will have these differences, and each will be different by imitating what is different in this way (for, as a matter of fact, even in dance, in flute playing, and in cithara   10
playing it is possible for these dissimilarities to occur as well
as in the case of speeches and bare meter). Homer, for
example, made them better, Cleophon similar, and
Hegemon the Thasian, who first made parodies, and
Nicochares, who made the *Delias*, worse. And in the case of
dithyrambs and nomes, someone might likewise imitate just   15
as Timotheos and Philoxenus did the *Cyclopes*.[20] And by this
very difference[21] tragedy too stands apart from comedy: the
one wants to imitate those worse and the other those better
than those now.

3.

Further, how someone might imitate each of these is a

16   *Spoudaios* has a range of meanings: good, earnest, serious,
     weighty, etc. It is an important term in *On Poetics* and will be
     translated throughout by "of stature."

17   *Phaulos* means low, base, paltry, trivial, etc. It will be translated
     throughout by "inferior."

18   See Aristotle's *Nicomachean Ethics* 1145a15–33 and 1148b15–34
     in Appendix 6 below.

19   See Aristotle's *Politics* 1340a14–b17 in Appendix 5 below.

20   We have omitted *gas* at 1448a15.

21   We have accepted Casaubon's addition so that the text reads *autêi*

third difference of these. For even if the imitation is in the
same things and of the same things, it is possible sometimes
to imitate when reporting (either becoming some other as
Homer does [*poiei*] as the same and not changing) or else to
imitate with all those imitating[22] acting [*prattontas*] and
being in action [*energountas*].[23] As we said at the beginning,   25
imitation, then, consists in these three differences: in
which, what, and how. So in one sense as imitator
Sophocles would be the same as Homer, for both imitate
those of stature, while, in another, he would be the same as
Aristophanes, for both imitate those acting [*prattontas*] and
doing [*drôntas*]. From whence some say they are also called
dramata[24] because they imitate those doing [*drôntas*]. It is
for this reason that the Dorians also make a claim[25] to   30
tragedy and comedy (For the local Megarians make a claim
to comedy as having emerged at the time of their democra-

---

    de tautêi têi diaphorai.

[22] Some editors believe that the phrase "those imitating" is either
corrupt or interpolated. Aristotle seems to be bringing out the
curious fact that, if one disregards exits and entrances, despite
being an "imitation of action," tragedy contains no action in the
literal sense. The definition thus refers to the plot as an action.

[23] Aristotle uses the verb *energein* here; its cognate noun, *energeia*,
is an important term in Aristotle, literally indicating something
that has its *ergon* (work, deed, function) within itself, that is,
something complete and at the same time at work or in motion.
See, for example, *Metaphysics* 9.1–6.

[24] *Dramata* are in the broad sense "doings" and in the narrower
sense "dramas."

[25] The word is *antipoiountai*, again a compound of the verb *poiein*.
It can also mean "to exert oneself over" or "to have something
done in return to one"; etymologically it might be construed as
"antipoetize."

cy.[26] And those in Sicily make a claim to it, for Epicharmus, the poet, was from there; he was much earlier than Chionides and Magnes.[27] And some of those in the Peloponnese make a claim to tragedy.) The Dorians make names the sign. For they say that they call their outlying districts villages [*kômai*], while the Athenians call them

[26] Aristotle discusses Megarian comedy at *Nicomachean Ethics* 1123a20–24: "The vulgar man spends a lot in small expenditures and strikes a false note in making a brilliant display, in feasting, for example, his picnic-guests on the lavish scale of a wedding, and in underwriting a comic chorus introduces purple in the parodos, as those in Megara do." The scholium on this passage runs: "It was usual to make leather skins as the screens in comedy and not purple. . . . The Megarians are ridiculed in comedy, since they also claim that comedy was first discovered by them, inasmuch as the one who started comedy was Susarion the Megarian. They are disparaged as vulgar and tasteless and for using purple in the parodos. Aristophanes, at any rate, in mocking them, says somewhere, 'No stolen joke from Megara.' Ecphantides the oldest poet of old comedy says, 'I shall not go through a song of Megarian comedy; I am ashamed to make a Megarian drama.' It is shown on all sides that the Megarians are the inventors of comedy."

[27] Epicharmus is mentioned in Plato's *Theaetetus* (152e1–5); Socrates is speaking about the Heraclitean thesis: "Nothing ever is, but everything is always becoming. All of the wise, with the exception of Parmenides, concur about this, Protagoras, Heraclitus, and Empedocles, and of the poets, those who are tiptop in each kind of poetry, Epicharmus of comedy, and Homer, of tragedy." He is also mentioned in Iamblichus's *Life of Pythagoras* (36.266): "Epicharmus too was one of the external auditors [of the Pythagoreans], but he did not belong to the inner circle. On his arrival in Syracuse, he abstained from philosophizing openly on account of the tyranny of Hiero, but he put into meter the thoughts of the Pythagoreans, making known their secret doctrines playfully."

demes, as if comedians or revel singers [*kômôdoi*] were so
called not from reveling [*kômazein*] but by wandering from
village to village [*kata kômas*], and driven in dishonor from
the town. And they say they name doing [*poiein*] *dran*, but   1448b
that the Athenians name it *prattein*.[28] About the differences
of imitation, then, both how many they are and of what
they are, let these things have been said.

4.

Some two causes, and these natural, are likely to have
generated poetics as a whole. For just as to imitate is natural   5
to human beings from childhood (and in this they differ
from the rest of the animals in that they are the most imitative and do [*poieitai*] their first learning through imitation), so also is it natural for everyone to take pleasure in
imitations. And what happens in the way we act is a sign of
this; for we take pleasure in contemplating the most pre-   10
cisely made images of things which in themselves we see
with pain, for example, the visible shapes both of the least
estimable of beasts and of corpses. [29] And the cause of this

---

28   The verb *dran* is common in Aristotle and in Attic authors gen-
      erally. This passage is the only evidence we have that it is of
      Doric origin.

29   See *On the Parts of Animals* 644b22–645a30 in Appendix 2 below.
      Consider with this Aristotle's *On the Motion of Animals* (701b18–
      22): "Imagination [*phantasia*] and thinking [*noesis*] have the
      power of [experienced] things [*pragmata*], for in a certain way the
      kinds of the hot, cold, pleasant, or fearful, when they are
      thought, are in fact of the same sort as is each of the things.
      Accordingly, men both shudder and fear by thought alone." See
      as well *On the Soul* (427b21–24): "Further, whenever we have the
      opinion of something terrible or fearful, we immediately experi-
      ence it, and likewise if the opinion is of something encouraging.
      And we are likewise in the same condition in terms of our imag-

is that not only is learning most pleasant for philosophers, but also for everyone else alike, although they share in it to a small extent. They are pleased in seeing images because in their contemplating there is a coincidence of learning and figuring out[30] what each thing is, for example "That's him!"[31] since if by chance one has not seen it before, it will not qua imitation [*mimêma*] produce [*poiêsei*] pleasure except on account of its workmanship or color or on account of some other cause of this sort.[32] Since to imitate is natural for us, as well as harmony and rhythm (for it is manifest that meters are proper parts of rhythms), from the beginning those most naturally inclined toward them,

15

20

ination, just as would be the case were we to contemplate in a painting the terrible or encouraging things."

30   The verb is *sullogizesthai*, literally "to think together"; it is cognate with our "syllogism."

31   Literally "that this [man is] that." This is a common idiom used to indicate a sudden recognition that what one thought something was is really something else. The first known occurrence of this expression is Herodotus 1.32 at the climax of the story of the meeting of Solon and Croesus, their conversation about who is the happiest of men; this is, in a way, the *logos* behind tragedy. Consider also Sophocles' *Oedipus Tyrannus* 1145, where a similar phrase precipitates the recognition and reversal of the play and his *Philoctetes* 261 where Philoctetes says, "I am that one (*hode eimi ekeinos*) whom perhaps you've heard of as master of the bow of Heracles." Immediately after he realizes that Neoptolemus has not recognized him through his own notorious, as he believes, sufferings. See also Sophocles' *Oedipus at Colonus*, 138; *Ichneutai* (fragment 102 in Diggle, *Tragicorum graecorum fragmenta*); Aristophanes' *Clouds*, 985, 1152, 1167; Plato's *Charmides*, 166b; *Hippias Major*, 296d; *Phaedrus*, 241d; *Symposium*, 210e, 233a. See also Aristotle's *Rhetoric* 1410b10–27 in Appendix 3 below.

32   See Aristotle's *Politics* 1340a14–b15 in Appendix 5 below.

advancing little by little, generated *poiêsis* from their improvisations.[33] *Poiêsis* broke apart along the lines of their own characters. For the more august were imitators of beautiful and noble actions and men of the sort that do them, while the meaner imitated the actions of the inferior, first making invectives just as the others made hymns and encomia.[34] Now, although we cannot say that anyone made a poem of this sort before Homer, it is likely that there were many. But if we begin from Homer, it is possible (for example, his *Margites* and poems of this sort). The iambic meter too came about in invectives as is fitting for them, on account of which even now it is called iambic because they

25

30

---

[33] See Pseudo-Aristotle, *Problemata* 920b29–921a6: "Why is it that everyone enjoys rhythm, song, and in general consonances? Is it because we naturally enjoy motions that are natural? The sign is that children as soon as they are born enjoy them. It is due to their character that we enjoy different manners of songs. And we enjoy rhythm because it has a recognizable and ordered number, and it moves us in an ordered way; for ordered motion is more akin to us by nature than disordered. Here is a sign: when we are toiling, drinking, or eating in an orderly way, we preserve and increase our nature and power, but if they are done in a disorderly way, we destroy and alter it. The illnesses of the body are disturbances of the order of the body that is not according to nature. And we enjoy consonance because it is a blending of contraries that maintain a certain ratio [*logos*] in relation to one another. Now *logos* is an order, which, it was agreed, was pleasant by nature. And the blended is naturally more pleasant than the unblended, especially if on being perceptible the *logos* in the consonance should maintain the power of both extremes equally."

[34] In Book 2 of Plato's *Republic* (372b7), citizens of the first of Socrates' cities make encomia to the gods; in Book 10 (607a4), men are included, for "hymns to the gods and encomia to the good" are to be allowed in the city.

used to lampoon [*iambizon*] one another in this meter. And
some of the ancients became poets of heroic meter and
some of iambs. Just as Homer was also especially the poet
of things of stature (for not only did he make other things   35
well but also dramatic imitations[35]), so also was he the first
to indicate the characteristic shape of comedy, making not
invective but a drama[36] of the laughable. For *Margites*
stands in an analogy: just as the *Iliad* and the *Odyssey* are   1449a
related to tragedies so is this related to comedies. Once
tragedy and comedy came to light side by side, each initiat-
ing a turn toward each sort of *poiêsis* in conformity with
their own nature, some became makers of comedy instead
of iambs, and others became producers[37] of tragedy instead   5
of epics, because the latter forms [*schêmata*] were greater
and more estimable than the former.[38] Now, to go further

[35]   The phrase *mimêseis dramatikas* might also be translated "imitations of action."

[36]   Or "action."

[37]   *Didaskalos*, here producer, also has the non-technical and much
more common sense of "teacher."

[38]   For an alternative sequence in the origin of drama consider Livy
Book 7.2–3.1: "In this year [365 BC] and the following, when C.
Sulpicius Peticus and Caius Licinius Stolo were consuls, there
was a plague. Nothing worth recording was done except that for
the sake of imploring the gods' peace, a *lectisternium* [a banquet
offered to the gods] was held for the third time since the found-
ing of the city; and when the violence of the disease was not alle-
viated by either human counsels or divine help, with minds over-
come by superstition, theatrical performances are said to have
been instituted among other ways of placating celestial wrath.
This was a novelty for a warlike people, though there had been
circus spectacles. The theatrical performance was a small thing,
as are almost all beginnings, and it was besides a foreign affair.
Without any song, without the performance of songs to be imi-

in examining whether tragedy is or is not by now sufficient
in respect to its kinds, in order to judge it both by itself in

tated, players, summoned from Etruria, danced to the tunes of a
piper, and gestured decently in the Etruscan manner. Afterwards
the young began to imitate them, spouting funny things among
themselves in crude verses, and their gestures matched their
speech. Once it had been adopted it advanced by frequent use.
The native born players, because a player in Etruscan is called
ister, got the name *histriones*. These actors no longer bandied
about among themselves a verse like to the Fescinine that was
extemporaneous and unpolished, but they performed melodic
saturae [medleys], with a song now written out for the piper and
with the appropriate gestures. After a few years Livius
Andronicus was the first to discard *saturae* and weave a story into
a plot. At first, he, just as everyone else, was the actor of his own
songs; but it is said, when he was often called back for an encore
he ruined his voice, and when permission was granted he placed
a boy in front of the piper in order to sing, while he acted out the
song with somewhat more effective gestures, since he no longer
had to use his voice. Afterwards, actors had songs sung in accordance with their gestures, and the only thing left for them to do
was to speak dialogue. When with this regulation of stories they
had turned aside from laughter and unrestrained joking, and play
was altered little by little into an art, the youth, once the performance of dramas had been left for the actors, began on their
own in the old-fashioned way to toss about among themselves
funny things woven into verses. These farces were later called
exodia [after-songs] and were mostly joined with *Atellanae* dramas. They were a kind of play taken from the Oscans [Atella
being a town in Campania where the Oscans lived], and the
youth did not allow it to be polluted by actors. It was thus established that the performers of *Atellanae* were not to have their
names removed from the register of the tribe to which they
belonged, and they should serve in the army just as if they had
nothing in common with the theatrical art.

   "Among the small beginnings of other things it was thought
fitting to set down the first origin of the theater, so that it might

relation to itself and in relation to the spectators, is another
account [*logos*]. But regardless of that issue, it came to be
from an improvisatory beginning (both it and comedy, one   10
from those who took the lead in the dithyramb and the
other from those in the phallic songs, which even now in
many cities continue by customary practice) and increased
little by little as they made advances in as much of it as was
evident to them.[39] After undergoing many changes, tragedy   15
stopped when it attained its own nature. Aeschylus was the

appear how from a sound beginning it has come into this kind of
madness that is hardly tolerable for wealthy kingdoms. Still all in
all the first beginning of plays, granted for the administration of
religious rites, did not relieve minds from religion or bodies
from sickness."

[39] Lucas cites a passage from Archilochus as evidence that this
leader, the *exarchôn*, not only led the chorus, but in improvising
new words in response to their traditional refrain, was an anticipation of the distinction between actors and chorus (*Aristotle:
Poetics* 80). In the absence of any ancient dithyrambs, Pindar's
Pythian 11 offers a way to understand how choral lyric could
have evolved into tragedy. There Pindar first recounts
Clytaemestra's murder of Cassandra and Agamemnon, and the
rescue of Orestes by his nurse (17–22), and at the end Orestes'
murder of his mother and Aegisthus (36–37). In between he asks
himself the question whether Clytaemestra killed Agamemnon
because of the sacrifice of Iphigeneia or her adultery with
Aegisthus, and accordingly whether Orestes had proper grounds
for killing his mother (22–25). Pindar does not answer this question; instead, immediately after he records Orestes' murder of
his mother, he turns to the chorus and asks whether he became
dizzy at the crossroads and abandoned the right path he was on
before. Pindar, in other words, duplicates the madness of Orestes
on the level of reflection rather than of action. It seems, then,
not to be an enormous step to translate Pindar's puzzle into a
mimetic action.

first to bring the number of performers from one to two, to diminish the role of the chorus, and provide for speech to take the leading part. Sophocles then provided three actors and scene painting. And further, because it was transformed out of the satyr drama from stories small in magnitude and   20
of a laughable way of talking,[40] it just lately got its august finish, while the meter, from having been tetrameter became iambic. At first they used tetrameter because the *poiêsis* was satyric and more suited for dancing, but once there was talking, nature herself discovered the proper meter, for iambic is the meter most characteristic of talk.   25
And a sign of this is that we speak mostly iambs in talking with one another, while we speak hexameters seldom and when we depart from the intonation[41] of talk. And further, the number of episodes increased. But as for the other things, how each are said to have been arranged, let them   30
have been mentioned by us, for it would perhaps be quite a task to go through them one by one.

5.

Comedy, just as we said, is an imitation of what is inferior to a greater degree, not however with respect to all vice, but the laughable is a proper part of the shameful and ugly. For the laughable is a sort of mistake and ugliness that   35
is painless and not destructive, such as for instance the laughable mask is something ugly and distorted, but without causing pain. The changes of tragedy and that through which they came to be have not passed unnoticed, but comedy because it was of no stature from the beginning passed   1449b

---

[40] *Lexis* is spoken speech and, except where particularly awkward, will be rendered by "talk." Here it is "way of talking."

[41] The Greek is *harmonia*, which has a range of meaning from "agreement" or "joining" to "scale."

unnoticed.[42] For the archon just lately gave a chorus of

[42] There is only fragmentary ancient evidence about the origin and
development of comedy. The following is in a fragment of a literary history (from Kaibel's edition of *Comicorum Graecorum
Fragmenta* [Berlin 1958], pp. 6–7: " They say that comedy was
discovered by Sousarion, and some say it got its name from the
fact that they used to go around singing and putting on a show
village by village, when there were not yet cities but men lived in
villages, but others contradict them and say they are not called
kômai among the Athenians but demes, and they call it comedy
because they used to revel in the roadways. They assert as well
that comedy is also called *trugôdia* because new wine, which was
called *trux* (lees), was offered at the Lenaion to those in high
repute, or else it was because when masks had not yet been
invented they used to smear their faces with lees when they
acted." And the following from a Scholium to Dionysius Thrax,
p. 14 (Kaibel): "The aim of tragedy is to move its auditors to
lamentation, the aim of comedy to move it to laughter. They say
accordingly that tragedy dissolves life, comedy puts it together."
{This remark is found in several other notices about comedy.}
And from Athenaeus (14.621D) on Doric comedy (Kaibel, 73–
74): "Among the Spartans there was a certain ancient form of
comic playfulness, as Sosibius says, not of very much stature,
because Sparta even then was aiming at the plain and simple.
One used to imitate with a cheap style of talk people stealing the
harvest or a foreign doctor saying the sort of things one finds in
Alexis's *Mandragorizomene*, . . . and those who practiced this kind
of play were called among the Spartans *deikelistai* (exhibitors), or
as one would say makers of theatrical props and mimes. There
are many different names in different regions for *deikelistai*. The
Sicyonians call them *phallophoroi* (phallus-carriers), others call
them *autokabdaloi* (improvisers), others *phluakes* (jesters), as
Italians do, and the many call them sophists. Semus the Delian
in the book 'About Paeans,' says the so-called *autokabdaloi* were
crowned with ivy and recited speeches slowly; but later they were
called *iamboi*, both them and their poems; but the *ithuphalloi*
(those with erect phalluses) wore masks of drunkards and

comic singers, but before that they were volunteers.[43] But only when it already had certain characteristics are those who are said to be poets of comedy remembered. And who assigned to it masks, or prologues, or a number of performers, and other things of this sort has remained unknown.[44] The making of stories came on the one hand from the beginning from Sicily, but of those in Athens, Crates was the first to make speeches and stories of a general character once he discarded the form of the lampoon.

Epic poetry follows tragedy as far as being an imitation of men of stature[45] in speech with meter, but in this it

crowns, with brightly colored sleeves [gloves?]; they wore half-white chitons, with a ribbon of diaphanous material that covered them up to their ankles. They entered in silence through the gateway, and on turning to the audience said, 'Get up! Make room for the god! He wants to go through the middle upright and throbbing.' The *phallophoroi*, he says, do not wear a mask, but they put on a visor of tufted thyme and chervil and a crown thick with violets and ivy. They wear thick cloaks and enter, some through the parodos and others though the middle door, and going in rhythm they say, 'We celebrate this muse for you, Bacchus, pouring out a simple rhythm for a complex song; it is novel and virginal, without the use of any previous songs, but we take the lead in an uncontaminated hymn.' Then in running forward they mock whomever they choose."

43 Aristotle *Constitution of Athens* 56.2–3: "The archon, as soon as he enters office makes a proclamation to the effect that everyone keeps and controls as much as he had before he entered office until the end of his rule. Next he appoints three *chorêgoi* (chorus-providers) for the tragic singers from the wealthiest Athenians. Previously he used to provide five for the comic singers, but now the tribes support them."

44 This is the passive of the verb *agnoiein* – elsewhere translated as "to be ignorant."

45 The Greek could also mean "things of stature."

differs: in having a simple meter and being a report. And further, they differ in length. The one tries especially to be bound by one circuit of the sun or to vary only a little from this, but epic poetry is indeterminate with respect to time, and in this it differs, although at first they used to do this   15
alike in tragedies and in epics. Some parts are the same, but some are peculiar to tragedy. For this reason, whoever knows about tragedy of stature and inferior tragedy knows also about epics. For what epic poetry has belongs to tragedy, but all that belongs to it is not in epic poetry.   20

6.

About the art of imitation in hexameters, then, and about comedy, we will speak later; but let us speak about tragedy, taking up the definition of its being that comes to be on the basis of what has been said of it.[46] Tragedy, then, is an imitation of an action that is of stature and complete,   25
with magnitude, that, by means of sweetened speech,[47] but with each of its kinds separate in its proper parts, is of people acting[48] and not through report, and accomplishes

[46]   "Being" translates *ousia*; elsewhere it is the first of the categories of being (*on*), that in relation to which the nine others are to be understood. (Aristotle also regularly uses it to mean "property" – the two meanings being related as are our "realty" and "reality"). Rarely does *ousia* occur in Aristotle of an artifact except by way of an example. Here it is particularly striking because it is juxtaposed with becoming. Aristotle nowhere else uses the phrase "the definition that comes to be" (*ho ginomenos horos*).

[47]   We have followed the suggestion by Professor Gregory Sifakis in a lecture at New York University that *hêdusmenôi logôi* is an instrumental dative.

[48]   The word is *drôntôn*, the present genitive plural participle of the verb *dran*.

through pity and fear the cleansing[49] of experiences of this
sort.[50] I mean [*legô*] by "sweetened speech" that which has
rhythm, harmony, and song, and by "separate in its kinds"   30
sometimes through meters alone accomplishing its task and
again at other times through song. And (1) since they do
[*poiountai*] the imitation by acting [*prattontes*], the ordered
arrangement of the *opsis*[51] would in the first place be of
necessity some proper part of tragedy. Next, (2) song-making and (3) talk would be as well, for they do [*poiouon-
tai*] the imitation in these. By the putting together of the
meters, I mean [*legô*] talk in the strict sense, and by song-   35
making I mean what has an altogether evident power. But,
since imitation is of action, and it is acted by some who
are acting who necessarily are of a certain sort with respect
to (4) character and (5) thought[52] (for it is through these
that we say actions also are of a certain sort, and it is   1450a

---

[49]   "Cleansing" is *katharsis*; Aristotle treats it at somewhat more
       length at *Politics* 1342a5–16. See Appendix 1f. Many believe that
       its definition dropped out after "through song" below.

[50]   "Experiences" translates *pathêmata*, which has the same root as
       pathos, translated as "suffering." *Pathêmata* also occurs at
       1459b11, where, however, it has the same meaning as *pathos*.

[51]   The Greek is *ho tês opseôs kosmos*. *Kosmos* means "order" or "*the
       order*" – i.e., the cosmos. It may also mean "adornment." *Opsis*
       (plural *opseis*) means primarily "spectacle" here, but may also
       refer to the faculty of sight or even to the visage (we have
       transliterated it throughout to preserve this range of meaning).
       Ho tês opseôs kosmos clearly refers, in the first instance, to the way
       in which the visible features of drama are arranged on the stage
       and includes such things as scenery and costumes but also the
       entrances and exits of the actors.

[52]   "Character" is *êthos*, and "thought" is *dianoia*; these terms are
       introduced by Aristotle at the beginning of *Nicomachean Ethics*
       Book 2 to designate respectively moral and intellectual virtue.

according to these that all are either fortunate or unfortunate), and (6) since the story is the imitation of the action, and thought and character are by nature the two causes of actions[53] (for I mean [*legô*] this by story,[54] the putting 5

[53] Following a tentative suggestion of Vahlen we have moved this clause – "and thought and character are by nature the two causes of actions" – here from 1450a1; this requires emending *pephuken* to read *pephuked'*. This change solves the puzzle of the strangely repetitive character of the text from 1449b6 to 1450a3 and also avoids a *men solitarium* at 1450d3. In addition it has interesting consequences for the way the argument builds toward the primacy of story among the proper parts of tragedy.

[54] The word is *muthos*; Aristotle uses it in a distinctive way here, for it means not only story or tale but also its composition. *Muthos* originally means "word," "speech," or "something said." Later it comes to mean "story" or "tale" and is opposed to *logos* – "rational account." It is significant that it is used to describe stories that deal with the gods. In *On Poetics*, Aristotle gives it the more technical meaning of "plot," while at the same time he diminishes the role of the divine in tragedy almost to the point of its disappearance. We have translated *muthos* as "story " throughout as a reminder of how radical an innovation Aristotle's understanding of plot is. *Muthos* as "plot" occurs nowhere prior to Aristotle. Elsewhere in Aristotle *muthos* has one of two meanings: either something remarkable or of a divine cause. On the relation of *muthos* to *logos* with respect to the divine and to tragedy consider the following excerpt from Plato's *Cratylus* (408b8–d2):
Socrates: And the likely, my comrade, holds Pan to be the double-natured son of Hermes.
Hermogenes: How is that?
Socrates: You know that *logos* signifies everything and is always circling and revolving around everything, and is double, true and false.
Hermogenes: Yes, of course.
Socrates: Isn't the case that the true part of it is smooth, divine, and dwells above among the gods, but the false dwells below among the many of human beings and is rough and tragic; for most *muthoi* and falsehoods are there, about the tragic life.

together of events,[55] and I mean by characters that according to which we say those acting are of a certain sort, and I mean by thought that by which, while speaking, they demonstrate something or declare their judgment), it is necessary for there to be six parts of all tragedy according to which tragedy is of a certain sort. And these are story, characters, talk, thought, *opsis*, and song-making. Two parts 10
are those in which they imitate, one is how they imitate, and three are what they imitate, and besides these there are none. Not a few of these parts have been used as virtually kinds of tragedy.[56] For even *opsis* has all [of tragedy], and in the same way it has character, story, talk, song, and thought.[57] But the greatest of these is the putting together of events. 15
For tragedy is an imitation, not of human beings, but of actions and of life. Both happiness and wretchedness[58]

> Hermogenes: Yes, of course.
> Socrates: Then rightly would he who reveals everything (*pan*) and is always (*aei*) revolving (*polôn*) be Pan goatherd (*aipolos*), the double-natured son of Hermes, whose upper part is smooth, the lower rough and goatlike (*tragoeidês*).

[55]   "Event" is *pragma*. *Pragmata* is "the business at hand," but the word, like *praxis*, derives from the verb "to act" – *prattein*. *Pragmata* therefore in some sense stand to *praxis* as do things done to the doing of them.

[56]   The sentence is clearly corrupt and as it stands is untranslatable; however the *megiston de* at 1450a15 suggests the sense, viz., that every part of tragedy may determine the character of a kind of tragedy but that the greatest of these is story.

[57]   Two of the five parts of tragedy listed here (character and song) have nominative forms identical to their accusative forms. Were the other three in the list also nominative the sentence would read as follows: For even *opsis* has everything, and character, story, song, talk, and thought have everything likewise.

[58]   "Wretchedness" [*kakodaimonia*] is the substantive equivalent of

depend on action, and the end is an action, not a quality.[59]
But human beings are of a certain sort according to their
characters but happy or the opposite according to their   20
actions. Therefore, they do not act in order to imitate characters, but they include characters because of actions; so
that the events and the story are the end of tragedy, and the
end is the greatest of all. Further, without action, tragedy
could not come to be, but without characters it could come   25
to be. For the tragedies of most of the recent poets are
characterless, and in general many poets are of the same
sort as, in the case of the painters, Zeuxis stands toward
Polygnotus. For Polygnotus is a good painter of character
while the painting of Zeuxis has no character at all.[60]
Further, if one places in a sequence declamations involving
character and well-made with respect to talk and thought,   30
he will not make what was taken to be the function of
tragedy, but the tragedy which has employed these ele-
ments to a lesser degree will do it much more if it has story,
i.e., the putting together of events. In addition to these

    kakodaimôn, which always carries with it the notion of contempt;
    it is extremely common in Aristophanes (89 times), four times in
    Plato (Apollodorus' use of it at *Symposium* 173d1 gives a good
    indication of its meaning), once in Euripides (*Hippolytus* 1362),
    and nowhere else in Aristotle.

59   "Quality" (*poiotês*) is virtually restricted in Aristotle to the
    Categories, Analytics, Physics, and *Metaphysics.* Apart from this sin-
    gle occurrence in *On Poetics* it occurs four times in the *Eudemian
    Ethics* in a discussion of character (1220b) but in neither the
    Politics nor *Nicomachean Ethics.* It is a word coined by Socrates in
    Plato's *Theaetetus,* for which he apologizes, for in the context it
    looks as if there is a pun on making (*poiein*).

60   Pliny (*Natural History* 35.62) says that Zeuxis painted a Penelope
    whose character he seems to have depicted. He also says that
    Polygnotus first opened the mouth and showed the teeth (35.58).

parts the greatest things by which tragedy guides the soul[61] are parts of the story, reversals and recognitions.[62] Further, a sign of this is that those attempting to make poetry [*poiein*], like almost all of the first poets, are able to be precise with respect to talk and characters earlier than they are able to put events together. Story, then, is the first principle[63] and like the soul of tragedy, and characters are second.

35

---

[61]   "Guides the soul" is *psuchagôgei*; it referred originally to the leading of souls into or out of Hades and therefore to a kind of sorcery and black magic. The adjective *psuchagôgikon* occurs at 1450b16 of *opsis*. Neither word occurs anywhere else in Aristotle. *Psuchagôgia* (leading of the soul) occurs twice in Plato's *Phaedrus* of the power of speech (261a8, 271c10). In Plato's *Minos* (321a4–5), Socrates says that tragedy is the most demos-pleasing and psychagogic of poetry. In the *Timaeus* (71a6), apparitions (*phantasmata*) occur by day and by night through the liver, which the god inserted in order to lead the soul. In the *Laws* (909b2–3), the Athenian Stranger speaks of atheistic sorcerers who in contempt of mankind enchant (*psuchagôgousin*) many of the living and claim to lead the souls of the dead. The scholium on Euripides' *Alcestis* 1128 says that there are Thessalian sorcerers called *psuchagôgoi* who by means of magical purifications lead back and forth phantom images, and the Spartans once sent for them when the phantom image of Pausanias terrified those who approached the temple of Artemis where they had slain him. In Xenophon *Memorabilia* (3.10.6), Socrates says that what more than anything else enchants (*psuchagôgei*) men through *opsis* is to make a statue appear alive. Strabo (1.2.3) says that Greek cities educate through music not for the sake of *psuchagôgia* but for the sake of inducing sobriety.

[62]   "Recognition" (*anagnôrisis*) occurs once at *Eudemian Ethics* 1237a25 and nowhere else in Aristotle. It occurs once in Plato. It does not occur in any other classical author. "Reversal" (*peripeteia*) occurs twice elsewhere in Aristotle.

[63]   *Archê*, elsewhere translated as "beginning" is translated here as "first principle."

(It is pretty nearly the same in the art of painting; if one 1450b
should smear on the most beautiful colors at random one
would not give delight to a like degree as one would were
one to give an image in outline.) In short, tragedy is an imitation of action and it is especially because of this that it is
of those acting. Thought is third, and this is to be able to 5
say what is the case and what is fitting, which is the same as
the task of the arts of politics and rhetoric in treating the
way we speak, for the ancients made them speak politically
and those now rhetorically.[64] Character shows up in the
choice that one makes.[65] Accordingly, there are speeches 10
that have no character, in which there is not in general anything that the speaker chooses or avoids. But thought is in
those speeches in which those with character show that
something is or is not, or declare something in general.
Talk is fourth, and I mean [*legô*] by talk, just as was said
before, the communication through language that has the 15
same power both in meters and in speeches. Of the rest,
song-making is the greatest of the things that sweeten,[66] but

[64] The tenth chapter of the tenth book of the *Nicomachean Ethics*
(1179a33–1181b24) goes some way in explaining the meaning of
this difference: to speak politically means to know the difference
between shame and fear, and between those who respond to the
noble and those whom the threat of punishment alone motivates,
and to speak rhetorically means to deny this difference in
natures, for speech is all-powerful, and to believe that legislation
consists solely in the collection of highly regarded laws. Homer
attributes the knowledge of the political way of speaking to
Odysseus (*Iliad* 2.188–205).

[65] We have followed the Arabic translation in omitting the phrase
en hois ouk esti dêlon proaireitai ê pheugei at 1450b9–10.

[66] Consider Plutarch's *Amatorius* (769C): "Just as poetry fits songs,
meters, and rhythms as sweeteners to speech (*logos*), and makes
the educative part of it more stimulating and the harmful part of

opsis, while it has the capacity to guide the soul, is the most artless part and least proper to poetics. For the power of tragedy is possible without a contest and performers, and further, concerning the production of *opseis* the art of the costume-maker is more sovereign than that of the poets.

20

7.

Now that these things have been determined, let us say after this of what sort the putting together of the events ought to be since this is the first and greatest part of tragedy. We have posited tragedy to be an imitation of a complete and whole action having some magnitude; for there is also a whole which has no magnitude. What has a beginning, middle, and end is a whole. A beginning is whatever in itself is not of necessity after something else but after which another [*heteron*] has a nature to be or to become. But an end, on the contrary, is whatever in itself has a nature to be after something else – either of necessity or for the most part[67] – but after it nothing else. And a middle is that which is both in itself after something else and after which there is another. Well-put-together stories, then, ought neither to begin from just anywhere nor end just anywhere but use the aforesaid forms. And further, since the beautiful, both animal and every matter [*pragma*] which is put together from certain things, ought not only to have these things in an ordered arrangement but also ought

25

30

35

> it less capable of being guarded against, so nature crowns woman with the grace of looks, the persuasiveness of voice, and the attractiveness of form, and while it enhances the allure of the unchaste, it equally assists the chaste in inducing the loving kindness of a husband."

[67] *Hôs epi to polu* – "for the most part" – is extremely frequent in Aristotle and often designates the natural.

to have from the beginning a magnitude that is not just
arbitrary – for the beautiful consists in magnitude and
order, whence neither could a very small animal be something beautiful (for its contemplation is blurred by coming
to be in an almost imperceptible time) nor could a very
great animal (for its contemplation occurs not at the same 1451a
time, and the oneness and wholeness vanish from its contemplation for those contemplating it) such as if there
should be an animal of ten thousand stades,[68] so that, just as
in the case of bodies and of animals they must have a magnitude, and this must be easily seen in a single glance, so
also in the case of stories they must have a length, and this 5
must be easily remembered. But limit of length that is relative to contests and the perception of them does not
belong to the art. For if a hundred tragedies had to be in a
contest they would be contesting against the water clock, as
now and then they say to be the case. But the limit according to the nature of the matter [*pragma*] itself is this: the 10
greater is always the more beautiful with respect to magnitude up to the point that it remains manifest all together.
So, if one were to speak so as to delimit it in an unqualified
way, an adequate limit of magnitude consists in whatever
magnitude a change occurs either to good fortune from ill
fortune or to ill fortune from good fortune of things that
come to be in succession according to the likely or the nec- 15
essary.

8.

    A story is one not as some suppose it is if it is concerned
with one human being, for countlessly many things happen
to one human being out of which, with the exception of

---

68   A stade is approximately 606 feet.

some, nothing is a one. So also the actions of one human being are many out of which no one action comes to be. Therefore, all of the poets are likely to have been mistaken who have made a *Heracleid*, a *Theseid*, and poems of this sort. For they suppose that since Heracles was one, it is fitting for the story too to be one. But just as Homer is distinguished in everything else, so too is it likely that he beautifully saw this, either because of his art or his nature. For, in making the *Odyssey*, he did not make everything that happened to Odysseus, such as his being wounded at Parnassus and making out as if he were crazy at the call to arms, of which it was neither necessary nor likely that because the one came to be the other came to be. But he put together the *Odyssey* concerning a single action in just the way we say, and the *Iliad* similarly. Just as in the other imitative arts the single imitation is of a single thing, so also the story, since it is an imitation of action, ought to be of one action, and this a whole. And the parts of the events ought to have been put together so that when a part is transposed or removed, the whole becomes different and changes. For whatever makes no noticeable difference if it is added or not added is no proper part of the whole.

9.

It is also apparent from what has been said that this too is not the task of the poet, i.e., to speak of what has come to be, but rather to speak of what sort of things would come to be, i.e., of what is possible according to the likely or the necessary.[69] For the historian and the poet do not differ by speaking either in meters or without meters (since it would

---

[69] This coupling of the likely and the necessary in a phrase is limited in Aristotle to *On Poetics*.

be possible for the writings of Herodotus be put in meters, and they would no less be a history with meter than without meters). But they differ in this: the one speaks of what has come to be while the other speaks of what sort would come to be. Therefore *poiêsis* is more philosophic and of more stature than history. For poetry speaks rather of the general things while history speaks of the particular things. The general, that it falls to a certain sort of man to say or do certain sorts of thing according to the likely or the necessary, is what poetry aims at in attaching names.[70] But the particular is what Alcibiades did [*epraxen*] or what he suffered. Now, in the case of comedy this has already become clear; for, having put together the story through likelihoods, only then do they support it with random names, but they do not make poetry [*poiousin*] about the individual as the makers of lampoons do. But with tragedy they cling to actual names. The cause of this is that the possible is persuasive. Just as, then, we do not trust to be possible things that have not yet come to be, so it is evident that the things that came to be are possible, for otherwise they would not have come to be if they were impossible. Nevertheless even in tragedies, in some, one or two of the names are of those known while the rest have been made up, and in some none are known, as, for example, in the *Antheus* of Agathon. For both the events and the names alike have been made up in it, and it delights no less. So that one ought not seek to cling completely to the stories that have been handed down concerning those whom tragedies are about. For to seek this would also be laughable, since even things known are known to few, but nevertheless they delight all. It is clear then from these things, that the poet [*poiêtês*] must be a maker [*poiêtês*] of

---

[70] Compare Plato's *Phaedrus* 271c10–272b2.

stories rather than of meters, insofar as he is a poet by
virtue of imitation, and he imitates actions. And he is no   30
less a poet should he happen to make what came to be, for
nothing prevents some of the things that came to be from
being the sort of things it is likely would come to be, and it
is in light of this that he is a poet.

Of simple stories and actions the episodic are worst. I
mean [*legô*] by an episodic story one in which the episodes   35
following one another are neither likely nor necessary.[71]
Tragedies of this sort are made by inferior poets on account
of themselves and by the good poets on account of the performers, for it is because they engage in [*poiountes*] compe-
titions and stretch the story beyond its capacity that they
are often compelled to twist the sequence out of shape. But   1452a
the imitation is not only of a complete action but of fearful
and pitiable things, and these come to be both especially or
more whenever on account of one another they come to be
contrary to expectation.[72] For if this is the case, it will be   5
more wondrous than if they come to be spontaneously or
by chance, since even among chance things those seem
most wondrous which appear to have come to be as if for a
purpose. For example, the statue of Mitys at Argos killed
the one who was the cause of the death of Mitys; it fell on
him while he contemplated it.[73] For it is likely that as things
of this sort do not come to be at random, so stories of this   10
sort are of necessity more beautiful.

---

[71]   Consider Aristotle's *Metaphysics* 1090b19–20: "On the basis of
       the phenomena, nature seems not to be episodic, as if it were like
       a poor tragedy."

[72]   *Para tên doxan* could also mean "contrary to opinion."

[73]   Plutarch adds that Mitys was killed during a civil war, i.e., his
       killer was not necessarily aiming at him.

10.

Of stories, some are simple while others are of a complex weave, for the actions, also, of which the stories are imitations, are from the start just of these sorts. And I mean [*legô*] by simple an action that comes to be as continuous and one, as we defined them, and of which the change comes to be without reversal or recognition, and by a tragedy of a complex weave, an action in[74] which the change is with a recognition or a reversal or both. And these ought to come to be from the very putting together of the story so that it happens that, on the basis of what occurred previously, these things come to be either from necessity or according to the likely. It makes a great deal of difference whether what we have before us comes to be because of what we have before us or after what we have before us.[75]

---

[74]   The Greek reads *ex* ("from" or "out of"), which the Arabic translation renders as "in." On the latter interpretation the change is a change that occurs within one action; on the former, it is a change that grows out of one action and results in another. The overall sense is not so different, and one is tempted to translate "out of" to preserve the parallelism with the genitive in the previous sentence on simple actions. However that parallelism is already fractured by the change of verb. Simple actions are those of which the change *comes to be* without recognition or reversal; complex actions are those in/from which the action *is* with a recognition, reversal, or both. Translating *ex* by "in" preserves this distinction.

[75]   This sentence is certainly perplexing. One expects a denial of the *post hoc ergo propter hoc* fallacy, and this is the way it is usually taken. See, for example, Lucas, 128, where it is likened to *Rhetoric* 1401b31 – *to gar meta touto hôs dia touto lambanousin*. Yet the dissimilarity of the passages is more striking than their similarity, for while in the *Rhetoric* Aristotle simply points to the error of taking "after this" to mean "because of this," here he says that the fact that *tade* (these things right in front of us) come

11.

What has been spoken of as the change into the contrary of the things being done is reversal, and this too, just as we say, according to the likely or necessary. For example, in the *Oedipus*, on his coming,[76] in supposing that he was   25
going to cheer Oedipus and release him from the fear regarding his mother, once he had made it clear who he was, he did [*epoiêsen*] the contrary. And in the *Lynceus*,[77] the one being led as though to be put to death with Danaus following as though to kill him, it turned out as a result of the things that had already been enacted that the latter was killed and the former saved.   30

Recognition [*anagnôrisis*], on the other hand, just as the name too signifies, is a change from ignorance [*agnoia*] to knowledge [*gnôsis*], whether toward friendship or enmity, of those whose relation to good or ill fortune has already been defined. A recognition is most beautiful when it comes to be at the same time as a reversal, for example as it is in the *Oedipus*. Although there are also other sorts of recognition

---

to be from *tade* differs from the fact that *tade* come to be after *tade*. The first *tade* is the problem, for it suggests that the same things are being spoken of throughout. One would have expected him to say that the fact that *tade* come to be from those (*ekeina*) differs from the fact that *tade* come to be after *ekeina*. The use of *tade* rather than *tauta* also emphasizes that these things that come to be come to be in relation to us. It seems, then, that Aristotle's expression is meant to recall, "That's him!" at 1448b18. On the two other occasions where *dia tade* occurs in Aristotle, *touto* precedes; *meta tade* occurs nowhere else. Plato has *dia tade* once and *meta tade* never.

[76]   At *Oedipus Tyrannus* 1002, the same verb refers not to the messenger's action in coming to Thebes but to his interpretation of the meaning of the action.

[77]   The *Lynceus* was written by Theodectes.

(for it is possible for recognition to occur in just the manner 35
that has been stated in regard to both lifeless and chance
things, and it is just as possible to recognize whether someone has acted or not acted), still, the one most characteristic
of the story and most characteristic of action is the one previously mentioned,[78] for a recognition and reversal of this
sort will have either pity or fear (we suppose tragedy to be 1452b
an imitation of such actions), and misfortune or good fortune will be the result of actions of this sort as well. Since,
in fact, recognition is recognition of some [men], some
recognitions are only of one toward another (whenever it is
clear who one of them is), but sometimes there must be a 5
recognition of both, as, for example, Orestes recognized
Iphigeneia from the sending of the letter, while Iphigeneia
needed another sort of recognition of him.

These, then, are two parts of the story, reversal and 10
recognition, and a third is suffering. Of these, reversal and
recognition have been spoken of, but suffering is a destructive or painful action such as killings in the open, and the
infliction of excessive pains and wounds and everything of
this sort.

12.[79]

We spoke before of the parts of tragedy which ought to
be used as kinds, but these are the parts separated according 15
to quantity and into which it is divided: prologue, episode,
exodus, choral part[80] – and this into parodus and stasimon.

---

[78] Literally, "the one having been said."

[79] Ritter and other editors have proposed the excision of this chapter.

[80] On the chorus see pseudo-Aristotle, *Problemata* 920a8–10 and
922b10–27 in Appendix 4 below.

These are common to all, while choral parts from the stage
and *kommoi* are peculiar to some. A prologue is a whole part
of tragedy before the parodus of the chorus. An episode is   20
a whole part of tragedy between whole choral songs. An
exodus is a whole part of tragedy after which there is no
choral song. Of the choral part, a parodus is the first whole
talk of the chorus, a stasimon is a choral song without
anapest or trochee, and a *kommos* is a lamentation common
to the chorus and those on stage. We spoke before of the   25
parts of tragedy which ought to be used as kinds, but these
are the parts separated according to quantity and into
which it is divided.[81]

13.

Following the things just now said, we have to speak
next of what we should aim at and what we should beware
of in putting together stories and on what basis tragedy will   30
do its job. Since, then, the putting together of the most
beautiful tragedy should be not simple but of a complex
weave, and what is more it should be imitative of fearful and
pitiable things (for this is peculiar to this sort of imitation),
first, just as it is clear that the sound[82] men ought not to be

[81] This last sentence of the chapter is almost identical to the first
with two exceptions: in the first sentence "these" is *tade* while in
the last it is *tauta*, and Aristotle may have used different forms of
the aorist for "we spoke," although the manuscripts differ here.
If he did use two different forms Aristotle might well be imitating within the Attic dialect the combination of Attic and Doric
dialects characteristic of choral odes. Throughout this chapter
Aristotle uses *meros* to refer to the parts of tragedy. The divisions
of tragedy in chapter six above are first introduced as *moria* –
proper parts.

[82] "Sound" translates *epieikês*. In Book 5 of the *Nicomachean Ethics*
(1137a31–1138a3) it is the virtue that belongs to the one who is

shown changing from good to bad fortune (for this is nei-   35
ther fearful nor pitiable but loathsome), so the wicked
ought not to be shown changing from misfortune to good
fortune (for this is the least tragic of all, since it has nothing
of what it ought to have as it is neither productive of a feeling of kinship with the human[83] nor pitiable nor fearful) any   1453a
more than the very evil man ought to appear to fall from
good fortune to ill fortune (for, though a putting together
of this sort would have the feeling of kinship with the
human, still it would not have either pity or fear; for with
respect to one who has ill fortune, the pity concerns his not
deserving it, and the fear concerns his being similar to us,   5
so that what occurs will be neither pitiable nor fearful[84]).
The one between these, then, is left. He who is neither distinguished by virtue and justice nor changing to bad fortune on account of vice and wickedness is of this sort, but
one who changes on account of some mistake and is one of   10
those in great repute and of good fortune such as Oedipus,
Thyestes, and notable men of families of this sort. It is

more just than justice, for he sees where the general rules of justice embodied in the law fall short in every particular case. The
epieikês is thus the man of equity. As one who in principle never
errs, he ought never to suffer for making mistakes. He is thus
especially unlike the man whom Aristotle praises for feeling
shame (*aidôs*) in Book 4 (1128b10–36) but only conditionally.
Shame is not a virtue, for it presupposes either that one has made
a mistake or could make a mistake that justifies one's shame.

83   The Greek is *philanthrôpon*. Aristotle discusses it once in the
     Nicomachean Ethics (1155a20) in the context of a discussion of
     friendship or *philia*.

84   The sense is that we pity those who suffer undeservedly.
     However Aristotle's language is a little odd here; in another con-
     text the clause might mean that he intends to discuss those who
     are unworthy (*anaxios*) and suffer a bad fate.

necessary, then, for the beautiful story to be simple rather
than, as some say, double and to change not to good fortune
from bad fortune but the opposite, from good fortune to   15
bad fortune, not because of wickedness but because of a
great mistake either of one such as has been said or of one
better rather than worse. And what happens is even a sign
of this, for at first poets were tellers of stories of any sort,
but now the most beautiful tragedies are put together about
a few families, such as about Alcmeon, Oedipus, Orestes,   20
Meleager, Thyestes, Telephus, and about everyone else to
whom it has fallen either to suffer or do (*poiêsai*) terrible
things.

Now, the most beautiful tragedy according to art is
from this sort of putting together. Hence also those who
accuse Euripides make the same mistake in saying that he   25
does this in his tragedies, and many of them do end in bad
fortune. For what he does is right as it has been stated. And
there is the greatest sign of this, for on stage and in the contests, those of this sort, if rightly done, appear most tragic,
and Euripides, even if he does not manage the rest well, yet
he appears still the most tragic of the poets. The second,   30
on the other hand, is the putting together which some say
to be first. It has the double putting-together, like the
Odyssey, and ends contrariwise for the better and the worse.
It seems to be first because of the weakness of the spectators. For the poets follow the spectators, making their poet-   35
ry as they would pray for things to be.[85] But this is not a
pleasure of tragedy but is rather proper to comedy, where
those who are the greatest of enemies in the story, for
example, Orestes and Aegisthus, having become friends, go
off at the end, and no one is killed by anyone.

[85]   Compare *Politics* 1288b23.

14.

Although it is possible for the fearful and the pitiable to come to be from *opsis*, still it is also possible from the mere putting together of the events. This is prior and character- izes the better poet. For the story must have been put together in such a way that, even without seeing, he who hears the events as they come to be shudders and pities from what occurs. This is what one would experience on hearing the story of the *Oedipus*. To provide for this through *opsis* is less artful and requires a subsidy. Those who do not produce through *opsis* the fearful but only the monstrous have nothing in common with tragedy, for one should not seek every pleasure from tragedy but what is proper to it. And, since the poet should produce the pleas- ure from pity and fear through imitation, it is apparent that a place must be made for this in the events. Let us then take up what sort of occurrences appear terrible and what sort piteous.[86] It is surely necessary that actions of this sort be in the relation of friends toward one another, or of enemies, or of neither. Should it be enemy toward enemy, he is nei- ther doing nor intending anything piteous except by virtue of the suffering itself, any more than if they are neither friends nor enemies. But the sufferings to be sought are these: whenever they come to be in friendships, such as if brother should either kill or intend to kill or do something else of this sort to brother, or son to father, or mother to son, or son to mother. The stories that have been handed down, then, are not to be loosened; I mean, for example, the killing of Clytaemestra by Orestes and of Eriphyle by Alcmeon, but he should be inventive on his own and use

---

[86] See *Rhetoric* 1382a20–1383a12 and 1385b11–1386b7 in Appendix 3 below.

these hand-me-downs beautifully. But let us say what we
mean more clearly by "beautifully." Just as it is possible for
the action to come to be in just the way the ancients made
it [epoioun], knowingly and with cognizance, and as
Euripides made [epoiêsen] Medea kill her children, so it is
also possible to act [praxai], and, being ignorant, to do   30
[praxai] what is terrible and then afterward to recognize the
friendship, just like Sophocles' Oedipus. Now this is outside the drama [drama], but it can be in the tragedy itself,
such as Astydamas' *Alcmeon* or Telegonus in the *Wounded
Odysseus*.[87] And further, a third besides these is to intend to   35
do [poiein] something beyond cure because of ignorance but
to recognize before doing it [poiêsai]. And besides these it is
not possible in a different way. For it is necessary either to
act [praxai] or not and knowingly or not knowingly. Of
these, to intend while cognizant and not to act [praxai] is
worst, for it is loathsome and not tragic, since it is without
suffering. Therefore no one makes it like this, unless rarely,   1454a
such as, in *Antigone*, Haemon toward Creon. Second is to
act [praxai], but it is better for the ignorant to act and, having acted, to recognize. For the loathsome is not attached
to it, and the recognition is astounding. But the strongest is   5
the last; I mean, for example, in the *Cresphontes*,[88] Merope
intends to kill her son and does not kill him but recognizes
him, and, in the *Iphigeneia*,[89] the sister goes through this
with her brother, and, in the *Helle*, the son, intending to
betray his mother, recognizes her. Because of this, as was
said some time ago, tragedies are not about many families.   10
For in seeking, they discovered not by art but by chance

---

[87]   The *Wounded Odysseus* is a lost play by Sophocles.

[88]   The *Cresphontes* is a lost play by Euripides.

[89]   Euripides' *Iphigeneia among the Taurians*.

how to produce this sort of thing in their stories . They are compelled, then, to have recourse to those families in which sufferings of this sort have occurred. Now, it has been adequately stated about the putting together of events and what sorts the stories should be.

15

15.

On the other hand, there are four things concerning characters at which one should aim – one and first that they be good. [90] There will be character if, on the one hand, the speech or the action, as was said, makes apparent some choice, whatever it is, and the character will be good if the speech or the action makes clear that the choice is good. On the other hand, "good" is dependent on the class[91] in which it is. For example, a woman is good and a slave is good, yet perhaps of these one is worse and the other altogether inferior. Second is that characters be fitting. For it is possible for a character to be manly, but it is not fitting for a woman to be manly in that way or to be terrifying.[92] And third is that character be similar, for this is quite another

20

25

---

[90] The word translated as "good" is *chrêsta*. It is cognate with the verb "to use" and always retains a hint of the good as the useful. It is the word Aristotle uses throughout this chapter. *Chrêstos* occurs once in the *Nicomachean Ethics* (1146a13) of desires, and twice in the *Eudemian Ethics*, but eleven times in the *Rhetoric* and five times in the *Politics* (in Plato *chrêstos* occurs some 100 times). Consider *Rhetoric* 1395b13–17: "All speeches have character in which the choice is clear. All sentiments [*gnômai*] do this because the speaker of a general sentiment makes a declaration about his choices, so that, if the opinions are good [*chrêstai*], they make the speaker appear to have a good character [*chrestoêthê*]."

[91] "Class" translates *genos*, elsewhere translated as either "family" or "genus."

[92] "Terrifying" translates *deinos*, which may also mean "clever."

thing from what was said before about making the character good and fitting. And fourth that character be consis-
tent. For even if the one who offers himself for imitation is
inconsistent and a character of this sort is presupposed,
nevertheless he should be consistently inconsistent. A
model of unnecessary evilness of character is like Menelaus
in the *Orestes*,[93] of the unsuitable and unfitting the lamenta-   30
tion of Odysseus in the *Scylla*[94] or the declamation of
Melanippe,[95] and of the inconsistent the *Iphigeneia at
Aulis*,[96] for she who supplicates is not at all like who she is
later.

Similarly, one must always seek in characters, just as
one also must in the putting together of events, either the
necessary or the likely so that it is either necessary or likely   35
for him who is of a certain sort to speak or do things of that
sort, and it is either necessary or likely for this to come to
be after that. It is apparent, then, that even the unravelings of

[93]   The play is by Euripides.

[94]   Neither the play nor the author is known,

[95]   This seems to allude to Euripides' *Melanippe the Wise* fragment
484 (Nauck): "The tale is not mine, but from my mother: Sky
and Earth were once one shape, but when they separated from
one another, they gave birth to all things and put them into the
light – trees, birds, the beasts the sea supports, and the race of
mortals." Another possibility is fragment 506 (Nauck), which
may be from the same play, but with Melanippe speaking: "Do
you imagine that injustices leap with wings to the gods, and then
someone writes them down in the leaves of the tablet of Zeus,
and Zeus, on inspecting them, passes judgment [justice] on mortals? Not even the whole sky would suffice were Zeus to write up
the mistakes of mortals, any more than he could, by inspection,
send the penalty to each, but Justice [*Dikê*] is somewhere here-
abouts, if you want to look."

[96]   The play is by Euripides.

stories should occur from the story itself, and not, as in the   1454b
Medea, from a contrivance[97] or in the *Iliad* the events sur-
rounding the sailing away.[98] But contrivance ought to be
used for things outside the drama, either whatever had
come to be before that a human being cannot know, or
whatever comes to be later which requires foretelling and   5
report. For we assign it to the gods to see everything. And
nothing irrational[99] should be in the events, but if there is,
it should be outside of the tragedy, such as in Sophocles'
Oedipus. Since tragedy is an imitation of those who are better than we, one ought to imitate the good image-   10
painters.[100] For, in rendering the individual shape, they
make them similar to it, but they paint them to be more

[97] In general, the word *mêchanê* means "contrivance," but in
tragedy it has the more specialized meaning of a cranelike device
used to lift gods into a scene from above – our *deus ex machina*.
The reference is to Medea's escape on such a contrivance on her
way to Athens.

[98] "Sailing away" might also be rendered "voyage back"; Aristotle
refers here to the intervention of Athena in *Iliad* Book 2 after
Agamemnon's speech has been misunderstood by the army, and
they scatter to their ships.

[99] The word is *alogon*; literally it means "without speech" or
"unspeakable."

[100] Homer's description of Agamemnon after the marshalling of the
troops (*Iliad* 2.478–9) – "He was in his glance and head like Zeus
who twists the thunderbolt, in his waist like Ares, and his chest
like Poseidon" – has this comment in the T Scholiast: "Painters
pursue the truth, the tragic poets the more august, and the comic
poets the less; all three are present in the poet, comedy in the
case of Thersites, painting in 'Automedon held the meat for him
and then glorious Achilles cut it' (*Iliad* 9. 209), and now in the
case of Agamemnon his appearance has been fashioned to be
more beautiful than the truth and more magnificent."

beautiful. So also, the poet, in imitating the irascible and
the easy-going and those who have in point of character
other traits of this sort, must in making them of that sort
make them sound, just as Homer made Achilles good and
the paradigm of cruelty.[101] These things should be closely   15
observed and, besides these, the visualization[102] that necessarily attends poetics. For it is often possible to make a mistake in regard to this. But enough has been said about this
in published accounts [*logois*].

16.

What recognition is has been spoken of before, but
there are kinds of recognition – first, the least artful, which   20
on account of an impasse they use most, the one through
signs. And of these some are natural such as "the spear
which the Earthborn bear" or the stars such as Carcinus
made in the *Thyestes*,[103] others are acquired, and of these
some are on the body, such as scars, while others are external to it, such as necklaces and such as in the recognition   25
through the cradle in the *Tyro*.[104] But it is possible to use
even these either better or worse. For example, Odysseus

---

[101]   We have accepted Lobel's emendation transposing *agathon kai* at
        1454b14. The scholium on *Iliad* 24.569 says that Aristotle assert-
        ed in his *Homeric Questions* that the character of Achilles was
        inconsistent (fragment 24 [149] Rose).

[102]   Literally "perceptions" [*aisthêseis*] (as in the following two sen-
        tences "this" is literally "these"). It is plural and includes not only
        what we see but also what we hear; of course we mean this as well
        when we say that we visualize the action of a work of fiction.

[103]   The Earthborn had a birthmark in the shape of a spear.
        Carcinus's *Thyestes* is possibly the same as his *Aërope*.

[104]   Sophocles wrote two plays called *Tyro*. There is a parody of the
        recognition in Aristophanes' *Lysistrata* (138): "It's no wonder
        that tragedies are from us (women), for we are nothing but

was recognized through the scar in one way by the nurse
and in another by the swineherds.[105] For all recognitions of
the latter sort, those for the sake of ensuring belief are less
artful, and all from signs are of this sort, but those that
result from reversal, like the one in the Bath Scene, are bet-   30
ter. Second are those the poet has made up, which are
therefore artless. For example, Orestes in the *Iphigeneia*
arranged for his recognition as Orestes, for she recognized
him through the letter, yet he himself says what the poet
wants but not what the story wants. Therefore it is some-   35
thing close to the aforesaid mistake, for it would have been
possible for him to bring something.[106] Also in Sophocles'
Tereus there is the "voice of the shuttle."[107] The third is
through memory, by the awareness that one has seen some-   1455a
thing, just like the recognition in Dicaeogenes' *Cyprians*,
for when he saw the painting he burst into tears, and the
one in the "tale of Alcinous"[108] for, hearing the lyre player
and remembering, Odysseus wept, from which they made
themselves be recognized. Fourth is the recognition by figuring out, such as in the *Libation Bearers*: "Someone similar   5

Poseidon and cradles" (i.e., women are good for nothing except
sex and birth). Poseidon was the father of Tyro's twin sons.

[105]   See *Odyssey* 19.386–502 for the nurse's recognition of Odysseus
and 21.205–25 where Odysseus is recognized by Eumaeus, the
swineherd, and Philoitius, the cowherd.

[106]   See Euripides' *Iphigeneia among the Taurians* 727–830.

[107]   The words seem to be a quotation. They refer, in any case, to the
picture that Procne's sister, Philomela, wove or embroidered in
which she depicted her rape by Tereus, Procne's husband.

[108]   This phrase designates Books 9–12 of the *Odyssey*, in which
Odysseus tells Alcinous about his travels (Plato, *Republic* 614b2;
Aristotle, *Rhetoric*, 1417a14). Odysseus weeps at *Odyssey* 8.521–
22, and this prompts Alcinous to ask him who he is.

has come, and no one is similar other than Orestes, so he has come after all."[109] And there is the recognition proposed by Polyidos the sophist about the *Iphigeneia*, for it was likely, he said, for Orestes to figure out that just as his sister was sacrificed, so it was also his lot to be sacrificed. And in Theodectes' *Tydeus*, he figures out that by coming to find his son he himself is destroyed. And also in the   10 *Phineidae*, for seeing the place, they figured out their fate, that in this place it was fated for them to die, for here also were they exposed. There is also a recognition put together from misreasoning of the audience,[110] such as in *Odysseus the False Messenger*.[111] But the best recognition of all is the one   15 from the events themselves when the astounding comes to be through the likely such as in Sophocles' *Oedipus* and in the *Iphigeneia*; for it is likely to wish to send writings. Only those of this sort, then, are without made-up signs and   20 necklaces. But second are those from figuring out.

17.

As much as possible one should put stories before one's eyes while putting them together and working them out together with the talk. For if one does this one would see most vividly, just as though one were among the actions themselves as they were being done, and would discover   25 what is appropriate, and one would least fail to notice incongruities. A sign of this is what Carcinus was criticized for. For Amphiaros was returning from the temple, which Carcinus failed to notice because he was not "looking" at it,[112] but on stage, it flopped because it annoyed the spectators. To whatever extent possible one must work it out with the gestures[113] as well, for those in the grip of experiences[114] on the basis of their own nature are the most persuasive,[115] and he who is under the stress of a storm induces storm stress, and he who is angry induces anger most genuinely. Therefore poetics belongs either to one with a good nature or to a madman, for of these, the former easily take any shape[116] and the latter are not themselves.

Regardless of whether they have already been made or he himself is making them, he must set forth accounts [*logous*] in general and then, on this basis, add episodes and stretch them out. And I mean [*legô*] the general would be contemplated in this way, for example of the *Iphigeneia*: A girl is sacrificed, disappears in a way that is not clear to those who sacrificed her, gets settled in another country in which it was the law to sacrifice strangers to the goddess, and she gets this priesthood. Later in time it happens that the brother of the priestess came, but that the god declared that he should go there for some cause is outside the general,

30

1455b

5

---

112 We follow Butcher in omitting *ton theatên*; Carcinus then becomes the understood subject.

113 "Gestures" translates *schêmata*, elsewhere translated as "characteristic shape."

114 *Pathê* is elsewhere translated as "sufferings."

115 Most editors read "on the basis of the same nature" and interpret it as saying that if two poets have the same nature, the one who duplicates the passion is more persuasive.

116 Or "easily mold themselves." For the relation between the poet and the madman, see Plato's *Ion* 535b–e.

and for what purpose he was to go there is outside the story. But on his arrival he was caught, and being about to be sacrificed, he made himself recognized (whether in Euripides' way or as Polyidos made it up in saying according to the likely that it was as it should be that not only his sister be sacrificed but also he himself), and from the recognition he was saved. It is after this that the poet must insert the names and make up the episodes, and he must make sure that the episodes are appropriate, for example in the case of Orestes, the madness through which he was caught and his being saved[117] through the cleansing.[118]

Now, in dramas the episodes are concise, but in epic poetry they are lengthened. For example, the account [*logos*] of the *Odyssey* is not long: Someone is abroad for many years, watched by Poseidon,[119] and he is alone, and further, the affairs at home are such that his goods are being used up by suitors and his son plotted against; having suffered through storms, he returns. After he makes himself recognized to some, on launching an attack, he himself is saved, and he destroys his enemies. This is peculiar to it; the rest are episodes.

[117]   In the play, Orestes is saved from being killed by way of a ruse that involves carrying a statue of Artemis down to the sea to be cleansed. However, the Greek *sôtêria* could also mean "restoration." This reading would allude to Orestes' restoration from madness.

[118]   Aristotle strangely omits the facts that Agamemnon sacrificed his daughter for the sake of the recovery of Helen, that Orestes killed his mother to avenge her killing of Agamemnon, and that Orestes' subsequent madness is caused by the pursuit of the furies.

[119]   Vahlen suggests replacing "Poseidon" with "the god," Ellebodius with "some god."

18.

Of every tragedy there is an entanglement[120] and an
unraveling,[121] the things outside and often some of those   25
within being the entanglement and the remainder the
unraveling. And I mean [*legô*] the entanglement to be what
is from the beginning until that part which is an extreme
from which it changes into good fortune or misfortune, and
by unraveling what is from the beginning of the change
until the end. So in the *Lynceus* of Theodectes the entangle-   30
ment is both the actions done before and the seizing of the
little child and again . . . but what is from the indictment for
the death until the end is the unraveling.[122] There are four
kinds of tragedy (for the parts also were said to be this
many): the complex, of which the whole is reversal and
recognition; the tragedy of suffering, such as both the
Ajaxes and *Ixions*; that of character, such as the *Women of
Phthia*[123] and the *Peleus*,[124] and the fourth . . . such as the
Daughters of Phorcus,[125] *Prometheus*, and whichever are in   1456a
Hades.[126] Now, in the best possible case one should try to

---

120 "Entanglement" is *desis*; it could also be translated "tying,"
"binding up," or "complication."

121 "Unraveling" is *lusis*, from the verb *luô*, to loosen or free; it also
has the sense of resolving, and later in the text even of analysis.
In chapters 25 and 26 it will be translated as "solution."

122 The text is corrupt.

123 A play by Sophocles.

124 Sophocles and Euripides each wrote a *Peleus*.

125 A satyr play by Aeschylus.

126 The text is corrupt. The fourth kind of tragedy is indicated by
the three letters *oês*. Bywater suggests *opsis*, Vahlen, the monstrous. See, however, 1459b8–9, which seems to indicate that the
fourth kind is the simple.

have all, but if not, the most important and as many as possible, especially since people unfairly criticize the poets as   5
they do now. For there have been poets good at each part,
but they claim that one poet ought to surpass the good that
is peculiar to each. But it is just to speak of a tragedy as the
same as or different from another by nothing so much as by
story, those being the same of which the weaving and the
unraveling are the same.[127] But many, while weaving well,
unravel badly. Yet both should be set in unison. And one has   10
to remember what has often been said and not make a composition that is characteristic of epic poetry into a tragedy
(I mean [*legô*] by epic poetry what is multistoried) just as if
someone were to make the whole story of the *Iliad* into a
tragedy. For there, because of its length, the parts assume
their fitting magnitude, but in dramas the parts are out of   15
line with this assumption. A sign of this is that all who made
a tragedy of the whole sack of Ilium, and not by parts like
Euripides, or of the whole of what happened to Niobe, and
not like Aeschylus, either fail or do badly in competition,
since even Agathon failed in this way alone. But in reversals
and in simple events, they hit the mark they want won-   20
drously, for this is tragic and has a kinship with the human.
And this occurs when the wise man with evil in him is
deceived, like Sisyphus, or the courageous but unjust man
is worsted. And this too is likely, for, as Agathon says, it is

---

[127] The argument here is so elliptical that Bywater suggests rear-
ranging the order of paragraphs. Aristotle wants to prove again
that the story is the most important of the parts of tragedy, this
time on the basis of its new division between entanglement and
unraveling. The digression on the four kinds of tragedy indicates
a certain concession to those who are critical of the modern
poets, but still, for Aristotle this is not the decisive issue; hence
the criticisms are unjust.

likely that many things come to be that are contrary to the   25
likely. The chorus should be understood as one of the performers, also as a proper part of the whole and sharing in
the competition, not as in Euripides, but as in Sophocles. In
the rest of the poets the singing no more belongs to the
story than to another tragedy. Therefore, the singing is just
thrown in; Agathon was the first to begin this sort of prac-   30
tice. However, what is the difference between throwing in
singing and fitting a declamation or a whole episode from
one thing into another?

19.

About all the other kinds we have already spoken, but it
remains to speak about talk and thought. Let the things
about thought be those established in the writings about   35
rhetoric, for this is more particular to that way of inquiry.
Those things fall under thought which are to be produced
by speech. The parts of these are proving, disproving,[128]
and the producing of passions[129] (such as pity, fear, or anger,   1456b
and all that are of this sort) and further aggrandizing and
belittlings. And it is clear that one should make use of the
same forms in the events as well whenever one ought to
produce pitiful things, terrible things, great things, or
likely things, except that it differs in this way, that the one   5
should be made apparent without being didactic, while the
other should be produced in speech by the speaker and
should come to be as a consequence of the speech. For
what otherwise would be the job of the speaker if things
appeared as they should and yet not on account of his

---

[128] The word is the infinitive *luein*, elsewhere translated as "to
unravel" or "to solve."

[129] *Pathê* is elsewhere translated as "sufferings."

speech? Of the things that pertain to talk, the figures of talk
are one kind of theoretical understanding, for example:
What is a command? and What is a prayer? and a narration,   10
a threat, a question, and an answer, as well as anything else
of this sort. This is for the art of performing to know and
for the one having an architectonic art of this sort. For with
the knowledge or ignorance of these, no criticism worth
serious consideration applies to poetics.[130] For why should   15
one assume that the mistake that Protagoras criticizes has
been made – that in believing that he prays, [Homer] issues
a command when he says "Sing goddess the wrath . . ."? For
it is Protagoras who says bidding to do or not is a command. Therefore, let it be passed over as a matter of theoretical understanding belonging to a different art and not to
poetics.

20.   20

The parts of all talk are as follows: letter,[131] syllable,
connective, noun,[132] verb, joint, deviation, speech. A letter,
then, is an indivisible sound, although not every one but
that out of which a sound comes to be put together by
nature. For there are also indivisible sounds of beasts none
of which I speak of as a letter. Its parts are the vowel,[133] the   25
semi-vowel,[134] and the mute.[135] A vowel is an audible sound

[130] Aristotle often distinguishes between the theoretical sciences
       (first philosophy or theology, mathematics, and physics) and the
       practical (ethics and politics), and the productive arts (*poiêtikai*).

[131] *Stoicheion* also means "element."

[132] *Onoma* may also mean "name" or "word." It will be used in the
       latter sense at the outset of the next chapter (1457a31).

[133] Literally "the sounded."

[134] Literally "the half-sounded."

[135] Literally "the non-sounded."

without the application [of the tongue to the mouth], while a semi-vowel is an audible sound with an application, such as the σ and the ρ, and a mute is with application, though it has no sound by itself, but becomes audible if it is with those having any sound, such as the γ and the δ. And these differ by virtue of the shapings of the mouth and locations, and by roughness and smoothness, and by length and shortness, and by the acute, grave, and intermediate. But to understand theoretically these things one by one is appropriate to the art of metrics. A syllable is a sound without significance put together from a mute and something having sound. For example, γρ without the α is a syllable, as well as with the α, i.e., γρα. But to understand the differences of these things theoretically also belongs to the art of metrics. A connective is a sound without significance which neither hinders nor makes one significant sound from being put together naturally out of many sounds both at the ends and in the middle, but which it is not fitting to put on its own at the beginning of a speech, for example *men*, *êtoi*, and *de*. Or it is a sound without significance which from many single significant sounds naturally makes one significant sound. A joint is a sound without significance which makes clear a beginning, end, or division of a speech, for example, *amphi* (around), *peri* (about), and the rest. Or it is a sound without significance which neither hinders nor makes one significant sound out of many sounds and is by nature put at the ends and at the middle. A noun is a put-together, significant sound without time, no part of which is significant in itself; for in doubled nouns we do not use a part as also itself significant in terms of itself. For example, in Theodoros (god's gift) the "doros" is not significant.[136] A verb is a put-together, significant sound with time, no part

30

35

1457a

5

10

15

[136] Compare Aristotle, *de interpretatione* 16a19–21: "A noun is a sig-

of which is significant in itself, just as also with nouns. For
"human being" or "white" do not signify at what time, but
"[he] walks" signifies in addition present time and "[he] has
walked" signifies past time. Deviation is of a noun or a verb.
One is with respect to the signifying of a thing, or to a
thing, and however many things of this sort there are, and
another is with respect to one or many, such as "human
beings" or "human being," and third with respect to the
things of performance, such as a question or a command.
For "Did [he] walk?" or "Walk!" is a deviation of a verb
with respect to these kinds. A speech is a put-together significant sound, some parts of which in themselves signify
something, for not every speech has been put together from
nouns and verbs, for example "the definition of human
being," so it is possible for there to be a speech without
verbs.[137] Yet it always has a part signifying something, such
as "Cleon" in "Cleon walks." And speech is one in two ways
– either by signifying one thing or as a connection from
several. For example, the *Iliad* is one by connection, but the
definition[138] of human being by signifying one thing.

20

25

30

21.

The kinds of word[139] are the simple (by simple I mean

nificant sound by way of being put together, no part of which is
significant if it is apart, for in *Kalippos*, *hippos* signifies nothing by
itself, as it does in *kalos hippos* [beautiful horse]."

[137] Compare Aristotle, *de interpretatione* 16b26–29: "A speech is a
put together significant sound, of which any of the parts is significant if separated, but as an utterance (*phasis*), not as an asser-
tion (*kataphasis*). I mean, for example, "man" signifies something,
but not that he is or is not."

[138] Following the Latin translation, we read *horismos* here, but even
were one to supply *logos* the translation would read the same.

[139] The Greek is *onoma*.

what has not been put together out of words signifying something, such as *gê*[140]) and the double. Of the latter, some have been put together out of a signifying word and a non-signifying word (except not out of a signifying [word] and non-signifying [word] in the word [put together]), and some have been put together out of signifying words. And there would also be a triple and a quadruple and a many-fold word, such as many words of the Massiliots, for example, *Hermo-kaikoxanthos*.[141] Every word is either ordinary, foreign, metaphor, ornament,[142] made-up, lengthened, shortened, or altered. I say ordinary to be what everyone uses, but foreign what others use; so that it is apparent that it is possible for the same word to be both ordinary and foreign, although not to the same people. For to the Cyprians, *sigunon* (spear) is ordinary, but to us foreign.[143] Metaphor is the application of a word belonging to something else either from the genus [*genos*] to a species [*eidos*], or from the species to the genus, or from the species to a species, or according to analogy.[144]

35

1457b

5

---

140 *Gê* is "earth."

141 This probably names a river; it consists of three proper names: *Hermos*, *Kaikos*, and *Xanthos*. There is a gap in the text here. From the Arabic "in-a-prayer-to-Zeus" has been restored as another many-fold word.

142 The Greek is *kosmos*.

143 Herodotus remarks that a tribe dwelling north of the Massiliots call retailers *sigunnai*, but the Cyprians use it for spears (5.9.3).

144 See also Aristotle, *Topics* 140a6–17: "Some things have been spoken of neither by way of homonymy, metaphor, nor common usage, for example, 'The law is the measure or image of the things just by nature.' Things of this sort are worse than metaphor. For metaphor makes what is signified somehow familiar on account of the likeness (for everyone in making metaphors does so in conformity with some similarity), but this sort of thing does not make it familiar, for just as there is no similarity in

By from genus to species I mean, for example, "my ship   10
stands here,"[145] for to be at anchor is a sort of standing. And
from species to genus: "Surely Odysseus has done ten thousand good things."[146] For ten thousand is many and in this
place it has been used instead of many. And from species to
species: for example, "drawing off the soul with bronze"
and "cutting with long-edged bronze."[147] For here "to draw   15
off" has expressed "to cut," and "to cut" "to draw off." For
both are a taking away. By analogy, I mean when the second
is to the first as the fourth to the third. For instead of the
second one will say the fourth, or instead of the fourth the
second. And sometimes they add instead of what it says   20
what is related to it. I mean, for example, a cup is to
Dionysus as a shield to Ares. Then one will say that the cup
is the shield of Dionysus and the shield the cup of Ares.[148]

accordance with which law is either a measure or an image, so it
is not usually said. Hence if one says by way of common usage that
law is a measure or an image, he is deceived (for an image is that
whose genesis is through imitation, and this is not characteristic
of law); but if it is not by common usage, it is clear that one has
spoken obscurely and in a way worse than anything said metaphorically." Aristotle seems to allude to Plato's *Statesman* 293e
and 300c–e, where the Eleatic Stranger says that the six defective
regimes (three law-abiding and three not) are all imitations of
the one right regime, and that the laws and writings of knowers
in each field are a second sailing and imitations of the truth.

[145] *Odyssey* 1.185. Athena, in disguise, is telling a false story about
herself.

[146] *Iliad* 2.272. The common soldiers are commenting on
Odysseus's beating of Thersites.

[147] These two are from Empedocles, fragments 138 and 143 in Diels,
H. and Kranz, W., *Die Fragmente der Vorsokratiker* (Berlin: 1954).

[148] See Timotheus fragment 2 (Page) from his *Persae*.

Or, old age is to life as evening to day; then one will say evening to be the old age of day as Empedocles does,[149] and old age to be the evening of life, or the sunset of life. For some of the analogies there is no word laid down, yet the similitude will be said nonetheless. For example, to scatter seed is to sow, while the scattering of the flame of the sun is nameless. But this is to the sun as sowing is to the seed, from which is said "sowing the god-made flame."[150] But it is possible to use this manner of metaphor also in a different way, to deny in one's designation of something that what is alien to it is one of its properties, for example, if one should say the shield is the cup not of Ares but wineless.[151] A made-up word is what, although generally not called so by anyone, the poet himself posits; for some seem to be of this sort; for example, horns are called branchings and a priest a pray-er.[152] And a word is lengthened or shortened, the former if one uses a longer vowel than is proper or an inserted syllable, the latter if any of it is shortened, lengthening, for example, *poleôs* [of the city] to *poleos* and *Pêleidou* [of the offspring of Peleus] to *Pêlêiadeô*, and shortening, for example, *kri* [barley] and *dô* [house] and "one *ops* [sight] comes to be from both [eyes]."[153] And it is altered when of the thing named he leaves part and makes up part, such as

25
30
35
1458a
5

---

[149] Fragment 152, Diels-Kranz, *Vorsokratiker*.

[150] Fragment of an unknown tragic or lyric poet.

[151] Modius posited a lacuna here to account for the lack of explication of ornament.

[152] The word is *arêtêra*; it is what Chryses is called at the outset of the *Iliad* (1.11). The suffix *têr* means that Chryses is a priest whose profession it is to pray on behalf of the people.

[153] The word shortened is *opsis*. The quotation is from Empedocles (fragment 88); it is quoted by Strabo.

"on the right [*dexiteron*] breast"[154] instead of "right" [*dex-ion*].

Of nouns[155] themselves, some are masculine, some fem-inine, and some in between. Those are masculine that end in ν, ρ, or σ, all that have been put together out of σ (these are two, ψ and ξ[156]), are masculine. And whichever end in those of the vowels that are always long, such as in η or ω, or, of those lengthened, in α, are feminine. So that those in which masculine and feminine end happen to be equal in number, for ψ and ξ are combined [with σ]. No noun ends in a mute or in a short vowel. But only three end in ι – *meli*, *kommi*, and *peperi* – and five in υ. And the in between[157] end in these and in ν and σ.[158]

22.

It is a virtue of talk to be clear and not low. That from ordinary words is thus clearest but low (the *poiêsis* of Cleo-phon is an example and that of Sthenelus), while the use of alien words is august and alters the idiomatic. I mean by alien the foreign, metaphor, the lengthened, and everything beyond the ordinary. But, were someone to make every-thing of this sort, it would be either an enigma or a bar-barism, an enigma if out of metaphors and a barbarism if out of foreign words. For this is the form of an enigma: while speaking of things that exist to join them together in impossible ways. One cannot do this in putting together

10

15

20

25

---

[154]   *Iliad* 5.393. Dione consoles Aphrodite for the wound inflicted on her, saying that Heracles once hit Hera on the right breast.

[155]   The Greek is *onomatôn*.

[156]   ψ is π + σ, and ξ is κ + σ.

[157]   The neuters.

[158]   Ritter brackets the final paragraph.

other words, but in putting together metaphors it is possible, for example, "I saw a man who welded bronze on a man   30
with fire"¹⁵⁹ and things of this sort. But when they are from
foreign words, it is a barbarism. There ought to be, somehow, a blending of these. For, on the one hand, the non-
idiomatic will make it not low, for example, the foreign,
metaphor, ornament, and the other species [*eidê*] mentioned, and, on the other hand, the ordinary will make for
clarity. The lengthenings, shortenings, and alterings of
words contribute not the least part to the combination of   1458b
clarity of talk with the non-idiomatic. For because of the
occurrence of the unusual and its difference from ordinary
talk, they will make for the non-idiomatic, but, because
they share in the usual, there will be clarity. So that those   5
do not rightly find fault who criticize this sort of talking
and make fun of the poet, as did Eucleides the old,¹⁶⁰ saying
that it is easy to make poetry if one is allowed to lengthen
to whatever extent one wishes. He made a lampoon in this
very style of talk: "I saw Epichares walking toward Mara-   10
thon."¹⁶¹ For, although it is laughable for it to be evident in
any way that one is using this manner, still due measure
[*metron*] is common to all of the parts. For, if one should use
metaphors, foreign words, and the other species [*eidê*] inap-
propriately and deliberately to raise a laugh, one would   15
accomplish the same thing. Observe what a great difference
the fitting makes if in the case of epic verse ordinary words

¹⁵⁹ An enigma of Cleobulina. Aristotle cites it at *Rhetoric* 1405a34–
b3. See Appendix 3 below.

¹⁶⁰ The identity of this Eucleides is not known.

¹⁶¹ The Greek is *Epicharên eidon Marathônade badizonta*. For it to
scan in dactylic hexameter, the initial epsilon and the initial alpha
in the last word would have to be lengthened. Aristotle adds a
second example, but the text is too corrupt to translate.

are inserted into the meter [*metron*]. Anyone replacing ordinary words with foreign words or metaphors or any other form would see that we speak truly. For example, Euripides made the same iamb as Aeschylus, replacing only one word, a foreign word instead of an ordinary and usual word; the one appeared beautiful, the other cheap. For Aeschylus in the *Philoctetes* made the line, "the ulcer which eats the flesh of my foot," while instead of "eats" Euripides has replaced it with "feasts upon."[162] And "being little, good for nothing and unseemly, [he blinded]," if someone replacing this should say ordinary words, "being now small, weak, and unattractive, [he blinded],"[163] or replacing "he put down an unseemly chair and a little table" should say "he put down a wretched chair and a small table,"[164] or replacing "the shore roars"[165] should say "the shore cries out."[166] Further-

20

25

30

---

[162] In fairness to Aeschylus, the verb *esthiein*, "to eat" or "to consume," is not used by Homer of human eating in the *Iliad* while the war is being waged until the last book, where Priam eats with Achilles; hence, Aeschylus *esthiei* is more strange or foreign than it looks. The verb *thoinô*, "to feast," does not in itself imply the act of eating. Aeschylus had used it for Prometheus' liver being feasted on by an eagle (*Prometheus* 1025) and Herodotus for the banquet Astyages makes of Harpagus's son (1.129.1).

[163] The quotation is from *Odyssey* 9.515; the context is Odysseus's blinding of the Cyclops. Aristotle's example involves replacing little (*oligos*) by small (*mikros*), good for nothing (*outidanos*) by weak (*asthenikos*), and unseemly (*aeikês*) by unattractive (*aeidês*). Our manuscript tradition has feeble (*akikus*) instead of *aeikês*, which in the context would have been much more suitable.

[164] The quotation is from *Odyssey* 20.259. Aristotle's example involves replacing unseemly (*aeikelion*) by wretched (*mochthêron*) and little (*oligên*) by small (*micran*).

[165] The quotation is from *Iliad* 17.265.

[166] The verb *krazein* is uncommon in the present tense; it occurs as the expressive perfect *kekragenai* mostly in poetry.

more, Ariphrades used to make fun of the tragedians because they make use of what no one would say in conversation, such as "from the house away" but not "away from the house," "thine," "and I him,"[167] "Achilles about" but not "about Achilles," and other things of this sort. For all things of this sort make for the non-idiomatic in talk because they are out of the ordinary. But he was ignorant of this. To use each of the things mentioned appropriately is a great thing, as well as using double and foreign words, but much the greatest is the metaphorical. For, just as it alone is not to be taken from another, so it is a sign of a good nature; for to make metaphors well is to contemplate what is like.[168] Of words, the double are especially fitting to dithyrambs, the foreign to heroic hexameter, and metaphors to iambs. All the things mentioned are also useful in heroic hexameter, but in iambs, because of the fact that talk is especially imitated, those words are fitting which one might also use in speeches, and the ordinary, metaphor, and ornament are of this sort. Concerning tragedy, then, and imitation in action, let what has been said be sufficient for us.

1459a

5

10

15

23.

In regard to the arts of narration and imitation in meter, it is clear that one ought to put together the stories just as one does in tragedies, so that in being dramatic, with a beginning, middle, and end concerned with one whole and complete action, they may make the proper pleasure just as one whole animal does.[169] And the puttings-together

20

---

[167] They use the pronoun *nin* instead of the more ordinary *auton*.

[168] See *Rhetoric* 1412a11–15 in Appendix 3 below.

[169] Compare Plato's *Phaedrus* (264c2–5): "But I suspect that you would say this, every logos ought to be put together like an ani-

should not be like histories, in which there is a necessity not to reveal a single action but rather a single time, everything that happened in that time about one or several people, each part of which relates to one another in a haphazard way. For just as the sea battle at Salamis and the battle against the Carthaginians in Sicily came to be at the same times, although not inclining to the same end, so also in successive times, one of the two comes to be after one of the two,[170] out of which not one single end comes to be. But pretty nearly most of the poets do [*drôsi*] this.[171] Therefore, as we said already, also in this respect Homer would appear "to speak in a divine way"[172] in comparison to everyone else in not even attempting to make the war a whole, although

25

30

mal, with a kind of body of its own, so as to be neither headless nor footless, but to have a middle and extremities that have been written in a way that suit one another and the whole."

[170] Under other circumstances one might translate *thateron meta thateron* as "one after the other," but here Aristotle has coupled the two in speech contrary to the expressed purpose of the sentence. The phrase *thateron meta thateron* implies that two "others" have been paired. The expression occurs only here in Aristotle, never in Plato.

[171] See Pindar's *Pythian* 1.71–80, where he links Hieron's victory over the Carthaginians and Etruscans with the battles at Salamis and Plataea through the notion of Greek freedom. He prepares for this by linking the barbarian with the monstrous, and the monstrous in turn with hatred of the Muses, who stand for Greekness.

[172] "To speak in a divine way" translates *thespesios*. The word is common in Homer, where it occurs thirty-five times, but it is rare in Aristotle, where it occurs only twice (the other time in a quotation). In Plato it occurs five times, always either in a quotation or meant ironically. Here Aristotle seems to use it to praise Homer Homerically.

it had a beginning and end. For the story would otherwise
have tended to be much too great and not easily seen at one
time, or, if moderated in size, of a complex weave in its
variety. But, as it stands, while he cut off one part, he used   35
many episodes of its parts and he divides up the *poiêsis* with
different episodes, for example, the catalogue of ships.[173]
But everyone else makes many-parted poems about one   1459b
man, one time, and one action, for example the poet who
made the *Cypria* and the *Little Iliad*. For this very reason,
from the *Iliad* and the *Odyssey* one tragedy is made from
each, or only two, but from the *Cypria* many are made and
from the *Little Iliad* more than eight, for example, *The*   5
Judgment of Arms, *Philoctetes*, *Neoptolemus*, *Eurypylos*,
Begging, *Laconian Women*, *Sack of Ilium* and *Sailing Away*, as
well as *Sinon* and *The Trojan Women*.[174]

[173] Vahlen cites the Scholiast on *Odyssey* 1.284: "Since the *Odyssey*
does not admit of itself an adequate complexity, he makes
Telemachus go to Sparta and Pylos in order that many Trojan
matters might be stated by way of digression through Nestor and
Menelaus, and now too one must state that the poet has made
the hypothesis itself of a complexity of speeches and variation of
forms in order that the tenor of the poem may not be uniform."

[174] In Proclus' *Chrestomathy* there is this summary of the *Little Iliad*,
from which one can see how closely Aristotle followed its
episodes: "Next there are four books of the *Little Iliad* by Lesches
of Mytilene; they comprise the following: the judgment of arms
occurs, and Odysseus gets them in accordance with Athena's
wish, Ajax goes mad, maltreats the booty of the Achaeans, and
kills himself; after this Odysseus waylays Helenus and, when he
has prophesied about Troy's capture, Diomedes brings back
Philoctetes from Lemnos. Philoctetes is cured by Machaon and
in single combat kills Alexander; and after his corpse has been
mutilated by Menelaus the Trojans pick it up and bury it; after
this Deiphobus marries Helen. Odysseus brings Neoptolemus
from Scyros and gives him the arms of his father; and Achilles'

24.

Furthermore, epic poetry should have the same kinds
as tragedy; for it must be either simple, of a complex weave,
of character, or of suffering. And the parts, except song-   10
making and *opsis*, are the same. For it too needs reversals,
recognitions, and sufferings, and its thoughts and talk must
be beautiful as well, all of which Homer was the first to
employ and to do so adequately. For each of his poems has
been put together – the *Iliad* as simple and of suffering and
the *Odyssey* as of a complex weave (for there is recognition   15
throughout the whole) and of character. And in addition to
these he has surpassed everyone in talk and in thought. But
epic poetry differs [from tragedy] with regard to the length
of its putting-together and its meter.

What has been said is a sufficient limit of length, for it
ought to be possible for the beginning and the end to be.   20
seen together; and this would be so if the puttings-together
were not as lengthy as those of the ancients but approached
the number of tragedies set for a single hearing. There is
something very peculiar to epic poetry with regard to the

phantom image appears to him. Eurypylus the son of Telephus
comes as a helper to the Trojans and Neoptolemus kills him
while he is proving to be the best. And the Trojans are besieged;
and Epeius, in accordance with the plan of Athena, fashions the
wooden horse. Odysseus mutilates himself and enters Ilium as a
spy; and on being recognized by Helen makes an arrangement
with her for the capture of the city, and after killing some of the
Trojans he goes back to the ships. After this he removes the pal-
ladion from Ilium with the help of Diomedes. Afterwards the
Greeks put their best men into the wooden horse and burning
their tents sail off to Tenedos. The Trojans, in supposing that
they are now free from evils, welcome the wooden horse into the
city and celebrate with a feast on the grounds that they have
beaten the Greeks."

further extension of its magnitude because in tragedy it is
impossible to imitate the actions of many parts being done   25
simultaneously, but on the stage the performers can have
only one part. But in epic poetry, because it is narration, it
is possible to make many parts be brought to completion at
the same time, by which, when proper, the bulk of the
poem is increased, so that epic poetry has this good with a
view to magnificence, to alter the disposition of the listener   30
and to introduce episodes that are dissimilar. For the quick
satiety of the similar makes tragedies flop.

As for its meter, the heroic has come to be a perfect fit
from experience. For if someone should make a narrative
imitation in some different meter or in many, it would
appear inappropriate. The heroic is the most stately and
weighty of meters (therefore, it especially welcomes foreign   35
words and metaphors, for, in fact, narrative imitation
exceeds the others in oddness), while the iamb and tetrameter are the meters of motion – the latter for dancing, the   1460a
former for acting. But it would be still more absurd if one
should mix them as did Chaeremon. Therefore no one has
put [*pepoiêken*] anything long together in a meter other than
the heroic, but, just as we said, nature itself teaches us to
choose what fits with it. Homer deserves to be praised in   5
many other ways, but in particular because, alone of the
poets, he is not ignorant of what he himself ought to do
[*poiein*]. For the poet himself ought to speak least; for he is
not on these terms an imitator. Now, all the others are
themselves the competitors throughout the whole, and they
imitate little and seldom. But he, after a little preface,   10
immediately introduces a man or a woman or some other
character – not one without character, but all having character.[175] Further, although one ought to make the wondrous

[175] Aristotle slides here from *êthos* as person to *êthos* as character; the

in tragedies, the irrational [*alogon*] is still more possible in epic poetry, and the wondrous is most of all a consequence of the irrational because we are not looking at the doer. Were the things concerning the pursuit of Hector on the   15 stage, they would appear laughable – men standing and not pursuing while one man signals, shaking his head – but in epic it is not noticed.[176] The wondrous is pleasant, and the sign of this is that in reporting everyone adds things as if to be gratifying. Homer has been especially effective in teaching everyone else how they must speak falsehoods; this is   20 the paralogism[177]. For whenever on this being so, this is, or, on this becoming so, this becomes, then human beings believe if the later is, the earlier too is or becomes. But this is a falsehood. Therefore, if the first is a falsehood, but if when this is, it is necessary that something else be or become, then one has to add the second. For on account of knowing this to be true, our soul misreasons that the first is   25 also. An example of this is from the *Bath Scene*. In short, impossible likelihoods should be preferred rather than possible implausibilities, and speeches should not be put together from irrational [*alogôn*] parts, but in the best

English "character" covers both.

[176] "And just as in a dream one cannot catch up with the one in flight, and neither can one get away from the other nor the other catch up, so Achilles was not able to take him in his course any more than he could avoid him. And how else could Hektor have avoided the fate of his death had not Apollo met him for the very last time and up close stirred might in him to make his knees swift? Achilles gave a nod to his head to the army, and forbade them to shoot bitter death at Hector, lest someone hit him and win glory and he come in second." (*Iliad* 22.199–207)

[177] *Paralogismos* was elsewhere (1455a13) translated by "misreasoning."

possible case they ought to have nothing irrational, and if
they do, it should be outside of the telling of the story[178] (like
the failure of Oedipus to know how Laius was killed) and   30
not in the drama (like the reports of the Pythian Games in
Electra or like the arrival at Mysia of the mute from Tegea
in the *Mysians*).[179] To say, then, that the story would be
destroyed is laughable, for stories of this sort should not be
put together to begin with. But if one does insert the irrational, and it appears rather reasonable, then the absurd too   35
is possible since it would be clear that the irrational things
in the *Odyssey* about his putting ashore would not be toler-   1460b
able if an inferior poet were to make them. But, as it is,
sweetening the absurd with all the other good things, the
poet wipes it out. And one should elaborate the talk in the

---

[178] "Telling of the story" translates *mutheuma*; the word occurs first
here in Greek and not again for two centuries.

[179] Compare Horace, *Ars Poetica*, 136–52: "Nor will you in this way
begin as the cyclic writer once did: 'I shall sing of the fortune of
Priam and the noble war.' How will he who promised this bring
out anything worthy of such great bombast? Mountains will be
pregnant; a ridiculous mouse will be born. How much more
rightly does he do who does nothing ineptly: 'Tell me muse of
the man who after the time of the capture of Troy saw the ways
and cities of many men.' He does not think to produce smoke
from flame, but light from smoke so that he might bring forth
from smoke brilliant marvels: Antiphates, Scylla and Charybdis,
along with the Cyclops. He does not begin the return of
Diomedes from the death of Meleager nor the Trojan War from
the twin egg. He always hastens to the event and carries the listener along into the middle of things just as if they were known.
And those things that he despairs of being able to make shine if
he treats them, he omits. And it is in this way that he lies. In this
way he mixes falsehoods with truths, so that the middle is not out
of line with the first thing, and the end is not out of line with the
middle."

idle parts and in those concerned neither with character nor thought, for very excessively brilliant talk[180] removes from view both characters and thoughts. 5

25.

Concerning problems and solutions,[181] it should become apparent by contemplating them in the following way both out of how many and out of what kinds they are. For, since the poet is an imitator, just as if he were a picture painter or some other maker of images, it is necessary that he always imitate some one of three things in number; for 10 he must imitate either: 1. what sort it was or is, or 2. what sort they say it to be or it seems to be, or 3. what sort it should be. And these are reported in a talk in which there are foreign words, metaphors, and many modifications[182] of talk. For we allow these things to the poets. In addition to this, the same rightness does not belong to the art of politics and poetics any more than to any other art and poetics. 15 But there is a double mistake that belongs to poetics itself – one is in itself and the other is the accidental. If his choice was right, but he fell short in the imitation on account of incapacity, the mistake belongs to poetics itself; but if his choice was not right, and a horse has at once thrown both right legs forward at once, the mistake has occurred in a particular art, for example, in medicine or any other art 20 whatsoever, and then it is not a mistake of poetics in

---

[180] This is an alliterative phrase – *lian lampra lexis*.

[181] "Solution" translates *lusis*, previously rendered as "unraveling."

[182] *Pathos* is translated as "modification" here; it is a technical rhetorical term. Elsewhere it has been translated in its more general sense of "suffering."

itself.[183] Hence one should solve[184] the problems the criticisms involve by looking at them on this basis. First, there are the criticisms directed against the art itself: "If it has made impossible things, it has made a mistake."[185] But it is right if it achieves its own end (for the end has been stated), if in this way it makes this or another part more astounding. The pursuit of Hector is an example. If, however, it was either more, or not less, possible for the end to exist even in accordance with the art about these things, then it has not rightly made a mistake. For it ought, if it is possible, generally to be without any mistakes. Further, to which of the two does the mistake belong? Is it according to art or according to something else accidental? For it is less if he did not know that a female deer does not have horns than if he depicted non-imitatively.[186] And besides this: if it is criticized because it is not true. But perhaps it is to be solved in this way: it is as it should be, for example, as Sophocles said he himself made men such as they should be while Euripides made men such as they are. But if in neither of these ways, it is to be solved in this way: "this is what they say," for example, the things about the gods; for perhaps it is neither better to speak in this way, nor is it true, but if it happened to be the case as it was for Xenophanes, still one

25

30

35

---

[183] There is a gap in the text in this sentence. We are translating Kassel's text with Vahlen's addition.

[184] The verb is *luein*, elsewhere translated as "unravel."

[185] We are translating Vahlen's emendation here.

[186] Aelian in his *de natura animalium* 7.39 cites several poets (Sophocles, Sophillus, Euripides, Pindar, Anacreon) who assigned horns to a female deer, and he goes on to remark that the grammarian Aristophanes of Byzantium weighed in on the side of the poets.

could say, "Well, they say, at any rate." And some things are
perhaps not better but were so, such as what concerns arms:
"Their spears [stood] erect on the butt end."[187] For they
had this custom then just as the Illyrians do even now.
Concerning whether something has been said or done by
someone beautifully or not beautifully, one must not only   5
consider whether it has stature or is inferior by looking at
what has been done or said in itself, but also at the doer or
speaker – in the presence of whom, or when, or in what
way, or for the sake of what, for example whether in order
that a greater good come to be or in order that a greater evil
be absent. But some problems should be resolved by look-   10
ing at the talk, for example, with respect to a foreign word,
"first *ourêas*";[188] for perhaps he means not mules but guards.
And with respect to Dolon, "he was surely bad in form
[*eidos*],"[189] he means not that the body is ill-proportioned,
but that the face [*prosôpon*] is ugly, for the Cretans call having a good face [*euprosôpon*] being well formed [*eueides*]. And
by "mix it livelier,"[190] he means not "unmixed wine," as if   15
for drunkards, but "more quickly." Or it has been said
metaphorically, for example, "then all gods and men slept
through the night," while at the same time he says "and yet
when at the Trojan plain he gazed . . . the din of flutes and
pipes."[191] For "all" has been said metaphorically instead of

---

[187]   *Iliad* 10.152.

[188]   *Iliad* 1.50. The rest of the line speaks of Apollo's plague attacking
        dogs.

[189]   *Iliad* 10.316. The rest of the line states that Dolon was swift-
        footed.

[190]   *Iliad* 9.202. In the previous line Achilles had urged Patroclus to
        bring a larger mixing-bowl.

[191]   Aristotle seems to have confused *Iliad* 2.1–2, where Zeus is said

"many," for "all" is a "much." And "she alone has no part"[192] is metaphorical, for the most known is the only one. And in terms of pitch variation, just as Hippias the Thasian solved "*didomen* to him to gain the boast"[193] and "the wood of which is rotted by rain."[194] And some are solved by division, for example Empedocles' "Quickly they grew mortal which previously had learned to be immortal, and pure previously to be mixed."[195] And some are solved by ambiguity: "*pleiô* two parts of night have past,"[196] for *pleiô*[197] is ambiguous. And some are solved by the habitual way of talking. They say, on the basis that a mixture [in the case of wine and water] is wine, there has been made a mixture of a

to be awake with *Iliad* 10.1–16, where all the other Achaeans were asleep but Agamemnon was awake.

192   *Iliad* 18.489. This is from the shield Hephaestus made for Achilles; it refers to the constellation of the Big Dipper.

193   *Didomen* with an accent on the first syllable means "we give" and with an accent on the second syllable is an infinitive with the force of the imperative, "give!" The reference seems to be to *Iliad* 2.15 where, however, we have a different text. Our source for this text is Aristotle's *Sophistical Refutations* 166b4–8: "and regarding the dream of Agamemnon, it is not that Zeus himself said 'we grant to him [*didomen*] to achieve his prayer' but Zeus was ordering the dream to give it."

194   Replacing *ou*, or "not" by the aspirated *hou* or "of which" – see *Iliad* 23.328. For this and the previous problem compare Aristotle's *Sophistical Refutations* 166b1–9.

195   "Previously" [*prin*] may govern either "pure" or "to be mixed." The reference is to Empedocles (fragment 35.14–15). Manuscripts of different authors cite the fragment in different ways.

196   See *Iliad* 10.252 – the problem is that Homer goes on to indicate that a full third part is left.

197   *Pleiô* means either "more than" or "full."

"greave of newly wrought tin,"[198] and on the basis that
those who work iron are workers in bronze, Ganymede has   30
been said to pour wine for Zeus,[199] although they do not
drink wine. But this might also be metaphorical. When a
word seems to signify a contradiction, one should look into
how many ways it might signify in what has been said, for
example, in "at this point the bronze spear was halted,"[200]
how many ways it is possible for it to be hindered – how   35
one might best understand it in this way or in that. This is
opposed to what Glaucon says people do: "Some men irra-   1461b
tionally have a preconception and then condemn what they
themselves have concluded, and they criticize as if someone
had spoken whatever they think is contrary to their own
belief." And the things concerning Icarius have suffered
this. For they believe him to be Laconian; it is absurd then   5
for Telemachus not to come upon him on his arrival at
Lacedaemon. But perhaps it is as the Cephallenians claim;
for they say that Odysseus married from among them and
that the man was Icadius, not Icarius. So on account of the
mistake it looks like a problem. In general, in relation to the
poiêsis, one should bring back the impossible either to what   10
is better or to opinion.[201] For in relation to the *poiêsis*, it is
better to choose a persuasive impossibility than something
unpersuasive and possible, and even if it is impossible for
beings of this sort to be such as Zeuxis painted them, still it

[198]   *Iliad* 21.592. Greaves were always made of a mixture of copper
and tin.

[199]   *Iliad* 20.234.

[200]   *Iliad* 20.272. The problem is that the spear is said to stop at the
layer of the shield made of gold even though the golden layer, as
ornamental, would certainly have been on the outside.
Aristarchus and others thought the line to be interpolated.

[201]   Others have understood there to be three possibilities here.

is better; for the model should exceed. The irrational ought to be brought back to what men say, both because they do so and because at times it is not irrational; for it is likely also that the contrary to the likely come to be.[202] One should look at things said in a contrary way, just as refutations do in speeches, to look at whether they are the same and in relation to the same thing and in a similar way so that it must be solved[203] either in relation to what he says or to what the prudent man assumes. Criticism is right both of irrationality and of wickedness whenever without any necessity one uses the irrational, as Euripides used Aegeus,[204] or one uses evil as in the *Orestes* Euripides used that of Menelaus. They bring criticisms, then, from five kinds – either as impossibilities, as irrationalities, as harms, as inconsistencies, or as against what is right according to an art. But solutions must be sought from the number of those mentioned. And there are twelve.

15

20

25

26.[205]

One might raise the question whether the imitation of epic poetry or tragic imitation is better. For if the less vulgar is better, and the one with a view to better spectators is always of this sort, it is very clear that the one leaving nothing

[202] This almost reproduces the quotation from Agathon cited at 1456a24 (chapter 18).

[203] Reading *luteon* for *autou* with M. Schmidt.

[204] In Euripides' *Medea* Aegeus is a character who comes in to offer Medea a place of refuge in Athens.

[205] The problems and solutions of chapter 25 lead in this chapter to the posing of the question about the relative rank of tragedy and epic; the theme of the previous chapter was "Homer never nods."

unimitated is the vulgar. Just as if they do not get it unless   30
the performer on his own makes additions, they indulge in
a great deal of movement as the inferior flautists do who,
when playing the flute, roll around if they have to imitate
the discus and, if they have to play Scylla, drag the leader of
the chorus around. Now, tragedy is in fact of this sort, just
as those earlier performers believed it of the later; for
Mynniskus used to call Callipides an ape because he exag-   35
gerated so much, and there was this sort of opinion also
about Pindar. But as these stand toward those, the whole art   1462a
stands toward epic poetry. The one, they say exists with a
view to sound spectators who require no gestures[206] at all,
but tragedy with a view to the inferior spectators. So if it is
vulgar, it is clear that it would be worse. First, this charge is   5
not made against poetics but against the art of performing,
since it is possible also for a rhapsode to be over elaborate
with signs, as Sosistratus did, and as Mnasitheus the
Opuntian did [*epoiei*] while singing. Second, neither is all
movement to be rejected, unless indeed dancing is also to
be rejected, but rather the movement that inferiors do.
This was also what was criticized in Callipides and now in   10
others because they imitate unfree women. Third, tragedy,
like epic poetry, does [*poiei*] its own thing even without
movement, for it is apparent through reading what sort of
thing it is. If, then, it is better in everything else, it is not
necessary that this, at any rate, belong to it. It is better first
because it has all the things that epic poetry has (for it is   15
possible even to use the meter of epic). Second, it has as
no small part music and *opseis*, on account of which pleasures are constituted most vividly. Third, this vividness
holds both in the reading and in the acting. Fourth, the

---

[206] Once again, as at 1455a29 "gestures" translates *schêmata*, elsewhere translated as "characteristic shape."

purpose[207] of its imitation is accomplished in a lesser   1462b
length, for what is more concentrated is more pleasant than
what is diluted in a long period of time – I mean [*legô*], for
example, if someone were to put Sophocles' *Oedipus* into an
epic of the length of the *Iliad*. Fifth, the imitation of the
epic poets is less a one; and a sign of this is that . . . many   5
tragedies come to be from any sort of epic imitation whatever, so that if they make one story, either it will appear cut
short by being shown briefly[208] or watered down by following the measured length. I mean [*legô*], for example, if it
should be put together from many actions, just as the *Iliad*
and the *Odyssey* have many parts of this sort which by themselves also have magnitude. And yet these poems have been   10
put together to be the best they can be, and as far as possible are an imitation of one action. If, then, it is distinguished in all these respects and, further, in what the art is
to do (for they should not make any chance pleasure but the
one that has been said), it is apparent that it would be better
were it to hit upon its end more than epic poetry does.   15

Concerning tragedy, then, and epic poetry – themselves, their kinds, and their parts – both how many they are
and in what way they differ, and what the causes are of their
being done well or not, and concerning criticisms and solutions, let so much have been said.[209]

---

[207] Elsewhere *telos* is translated as "end."

[208] The word is *muouros*; it means literally "mouse-tailed" and is
usually applied to certain kinds of fish; in *Rhetoric* 1409b18 it is
applied to periods. In the same place Aristotle uses *hudares*,
which we have translated as "watered down"; it is usually used of
diluted wine. At Aeschylus's *Agamemnon* 798 it is used metaphorically of friendship; it is also applied to friendship at *Politics*
1262b15.

[209] In the Florentine manuscript B, the Riccardianus, there follows

a sentence of which only a few letters are legible, but it might have said: "But about lampoons and comedy I shall not write." If this was the remark of the scribe and not of Aristotle, it would imply that he had before him the whole or part of the second book, for in the catalogue that we have of Aristotle's writings, *On Poetics* is listed with two books.

Appendices

1. References to *On Poetics* in other texts of Aristotle[1]

a. Aristotle *Rhetoric* 1.11, 1371b33: And likewise too since play and every relaxation is one of the pleasant things, and laughter is of the

---

[1] Compare also Proclus, *On Plato's* Republic 1:

> We have to say second why exactly does Plato not accept tragedy and comedy, despite the fact that they contribute to the purification [*aphosiôsis*] of the passions, which it is neither possible to lock out entirely nor safe to satisfy, but they need a certain opportune motion, which on being satisfied in the hearing of these [tragedy and comedy] makes us not be bothered by them in the future . . . . (Kroll, 42)

as well as:

> And the second problem, which we shall solve in a way that agrees with what we said before, was the oddity of rejecting tragedy and comedy, if, that is, it is possible through them to satisfy the passions in a moderate way and, once they are satisfied, make them amenable to education by treatment of the distress they cause – it has at any rate offered Aristotle a great opportunity for blame as well as those who argued on behalf of the poets against the speeches of Plato . . . . (Kroll, 49)

and:

> We too shall say that the statesman must devise a certain disgorging of these passions, but not so as to enhance the passionate attachment to them, but rather, on the contrary, to bridle them and pull back on their motions in a harmonious way; but those sorts of poetry that in addition to complexity have the unmeasured in them from their provocation of these passions are far from useful for purification [*aphosiôsis*]. (Kroll, 50)

See also Iamblichus, *On the Mysteries* 1.11:

> The powers of the human passions in us, if they are constrained on all sides, become more intense, but if they are brought forward for a brief activity [*energeia*] and up to the commensurate point are enjoyed in a measured way and satisfied, and then afterwards cleansed off by persuasion

pleasant things, it is necessary that the laughable things too be pleasant – human beings, speeches, and deeds; and there has been a separate treatment about laughable things in *On Poetics.*

b. *Rhetoric* 3.18, 1419b2: And about the laughable things, since they are thought to have some use in debates, and Gorgias said rightly that one must destroy the seriousness of one's opponents by laughter, and their laughter by seriousness, it has been stated in *On Poetics* as to how many kinds of laughable things there are, some of which suit the free man, and some do not. Irony is more characteristic of a free man than buffoonery, for the former invents [makes] the laughable about himself, but the buffoon about another.[2]

c. *Rhetoric* 3.2, 1404b37: Of names, whereas homonyms are useful for the sophist (for he does damage on account of them), synonyms are for the poet. I mean names that are in common use and synonymous, for example, *poreuesthai* (to go) and *badizein* (to walk), for both of these are in common use and synonyms of one another. Now what each of them is and how many kinds of metaphor there are and that this has the most effect both in poetry and in speeches, that is, metaphors, has been stated in *On Poetics* in just the way we were speaking about it.

d. Simplicius in his commentary on Aristotle's *Categories* 36.13: For in fact Aristotle in *On Poetics* said that synonyms are of those things for which there are several names but the same account [*logos*], just as are "polynyms," *lopion, himation,* and *pharos* [all words for cloak].

e. Antiatticist in Bekker's *Anecdota* 101.32: *kuntaton* (most shameless): Aristotle in *On Poetics*: "and the most shameless thing of all."[3]

> and not violently, then they do come to rest. On account of this, when we observe the passions of others in comedy and tragedy, we put a check on our own, make them more moderate, and cleanse them off.

[2]   See also *Nicomachean Ethics* 1.14 (1127b33-1128b9).

[3]   Since *kuntaton* has the root for dog (*kuôn)* in it, this quotation would have occurred in the discussion of metaphor.

f. Aristotle *Politics* 8.7, 1341b32: And since we accept the division of songs as some of those engaged in philosophy divide them, when they set down some of them as ethical, some practical, and some enthusiastic, and they also arrange the nature of scales in relation to their suitability to each of them, different for different songs, and since we assert that one must not use music for the sake of a single benefit but for several (for it is for the sake of education and cleansing – and what we mean by cleansing, we will now speak of in an unqualified way, but again in *On Poetics* more clearly – and thirdly as a pastime, for relaxation and rest from toils), it is evident that one must use all the scales, but one must not use them all in the same manner, but the most ethical scales for education, and, when others are performing, for listening, [one must use] the practical and enthusiastic scales. For whatever experience occurs strongly in the case of some souls, it is there from the start in all souls, and it just differs by the less and more, for example, pity and fear, and further enthusiasm; for by this latter kind of motion some are possessed, and whenever they use the songs that excite the soul to a frenzy, we see them get into this state from sacred songs and obtain as it were a medical cure and cleansing. It is necessary that those liable to pity and those liable to fear, as well as those who are in general easily affected, experience[4] this same thing, and everyone else does too to the extent that experiences of this sort befall each, and in the case of all a certain cleansing occurs and a lightening with pleasure. In the same way too cleansing [purificatory][5] songs provide a harmless joy to human beings.

g. Aristotle *Politics* 8.6, 1341a21: Furthermore the flute is not ethical but rather designed for exciting frenzy, so one must use it on those

---

[4] "Affected" [*pathêtikous*] is cognate with the verb "to experience" or "to suffer" [*paschein*].

[5] Sauppe and Ross read *ta melê ta praktika*—songs of action.

sorts of occasions in which contemplation [*theôria*] has a power to cleanse rather than to teach.

h. Aristotle *Politics* 8.5, 1340a5: [One has] to see as well whether at some point music pertains to character and the soul. This would be clear if we become of a certain sort through it. But that we do so become is evident through not only many other things but also through the songs of Olympus,[6] for it is agreed that these songs make souls enthusiastic, and enthusiasm is an experience of character of the soul. And further, when they listen to imitations, all share in the same affect, even apart from rhythms and songs.

2. Aristotle *On the Parts of Animals* 644b22–645a30:
Of the beings, all that are by nature, some do not come into being or perish for all of time, and others partake of generation and corruption. It turns out that the contemplation of those beings that are estimable and divine is less available to us from the start (for the things that are evident to perception are absolutely very few on the basis of which one would investigate them and about which we long to know); but in regard to corruptible plants and animals, we are

---

6   Two passages in Plato make clear what Aristotle means by enthusiasm, or literally "the state of having the gods within." Alcibiades in the *Symposium* (215b8–c6), in confirming the truth of his likening Socrates to the satyr Marsyas, says: "Well, aren't you a flute player? Yes you are, and far more amazing than he, inasmuch as he used to enchant human beings through instruments by the power from the mouth, and still even now everyone does it who plays his songs on the flute – for the songs which Olympus used to play on the flute were Marsyas's, for he was his teacher – regardless of whether a good flute player or a poor flute girl plays them, these songs alone make for possession and reveal those who are in need of the gods and initiatory rites because they are divine." In the *Minos* (317b4 b4–c1), Socrates says the flute songs are Marsyas's and Olympus's, "and they alone move and reveal those who are in need of the gods; and further they alone are left, inasmuch as they are divine."

better equipped for knowing them on account of our living with them. If one should want to take sufficient trouble one would grasp many of the things that are there in the case of each genus. Each of the two has its charm. Even if we should get hold of little in the former case, all the same, on account of the high rank in the knowledge, it would be more pleasant than all the things in our midst, just as in the case of those loved it is more pleasant to catch a glimpse of some ordinary and small part of them than to see with precision many other great things; but, on the other hand, the things in our midst, because more of them are better known, have the advantage in point of scientific knowledge. Furthermore, because they are nearer to us and more akin to our own nature, there is a sort of compensation in that in comparison with the philosophy that deals with the divine things. Since we already went through them in speaking of what appears to us, it remains to speak of animal nature, without the omission of anything as far as possible and regardless of whether it is more or less estimable. For even among things that lack charm in point of our perception of them, all the same in point of contemplation the craftsmanship of nature affords indescribable pleasures to those who are able to know their causes and are philosophic by nature. For it would be against all reason and strange, if we enjoy contemplating their images because we contemplate simultaneously the craftsmanship of art (the art of painting or sculpture for example), but in the case of their composition by nature we should not welcome even more their contemplation, provided that is we should be able to catch sight of their causes. Therefore one must not express disgust at the examination of the less estimable animals, for there is something wonderful in all natural things. It is just as Heraclitus is said to have said to strangers who wanted to meet him; when they approached and saw him warming himself at the stove they stopped; but he urged them to enter and have no fear, for he said, "Gods are also here." It is in just this way that one ought to approach the investigation of each of the

animals, without any sign of abashment, on the grounds that in all
of them there is something natural and beautiful. It is especially in
the works of nature that there is nothing random but rather that
which is for the sake of something. That which has been put together or has come into being for the sake of some end has occupied the
place of the beautiful. If someone maintains that the contemplation
of all other animals is not estimable, then one has to believe in the
same way about oneself, for it is not possible to see without much
disgust from what the race of human beings has been put together,
for example, blood, flesh, bones, veins, and parts of this sort.

3. Aristotle *Rhetoric*
1371b4–10:
Since to learn and to wonder are pleasant, it is necessary that the
following sorts of things be pleasant too, e.g., the imitated, just as
painting, sculpture, and poetics do, and everything that has been
well imitated, even if what has been imitated is not pleasant, for one
does not enjoy that, but rather there is a syllogism, "That's it!" and
the result is that one learns something.

1382a20–1383a12:
It will be evident in the following what sorts of things and of whom
men are afraid, and what their own state is when they are afraid. Let
fear be a certain pain or disturbance from the imagination [*phanta-
sia*] of a future evil, either destructive or painful. For men do not
fear all evil things, for example, whether he will be unjust or slow,
but all that signify great pains or corruptions, and these moreover if
they appear not far off but appear near enough to be imminent. For
men are not afraid of things that are very far off; all know that they
will die, but because it is not near, they show absolutely no concern.
So if fear is this, it is necessary that those things be fearful that
appear to have a great power to corrupt or inflict injuries that lead
to great pain. Accordingly even the signs of these are fearful, for the

fearful appears near at hand, and this is what danger is, the approaching of the fearful.

Enmity and anger of those who have the power to do some harm are of this sort (for it is clear that they want to and have the power, and hence they are close to doing it), and injustice if it is with power, for the unjust is unjust by choice. And insulted virtue if it has the power (for it is clear that it always chooses to act whenever it is insulted, and now it has the power); and fear of those who have the power to do some harm; for it is a necessity that a man like that be at the ready; and since the many are subject and enslaved to profiteering and are cowardly in dangers, to be in the power of another is for the most part frightening, and hence those who have secret knowledge of someone's terrible deed are to be feared either as informers or deserters; and those who are able to do wrong are frightening to those who are capable of being wronged; for human beings do wrong for the most part whenever they have the power. And those who have been wronged or believe they are wronged; for they are always on the lookout for an opportunity. And those who have done wrong, if they have the power, are frightening, because they are afraid of retaliation; for the fearful has been presupposed to be of this sort. And those who are rivals for the same things, everything that it is not possible for both to have at the same time; for they are always at war with those of that sort. And those who are frightening to those who are stronger than themselves, for they would be more capable of harming them, if they can harm the stronger. And whomever the stronger fear, for the same reason. And those who have killed those stronger than themselves, and those who attack those weaker than themselves, for either they are already frightening or they are on the increase. And of those who have been wronged and are enemies or rivals, it is not those quick to anger and are outspoken who are to be feared, but the gentle, the ironic, and criminally inclined; for just as it is not obvious whether they are close to acting, so it is never plain that they are far off. All things

that are frightening are more frightening when it is not possible to
rectify the mistakes they make, but either it is absolutely impossible
or it is not in their power but in the power of their opponents. And
for whomever help is not available or it is not easy. So, to speak
without qualification, all things are frightening if when they happen
or are about to happen to others they are pitiable.

Now the greatest of frightening things and what men are afraid
of are pretty nearly these; but now let us speak of what the disposition of men is when they are afraid. If fear accompanies an expectation that one will suffer some destructive experience, it is evident
that no one who believes he would not suffer anything is afraid, any
more than of those things which they believe they would not suffer
or of those by whom they believe they would not suffer, or at that
time when they believe they would not. It is necessary then that
those who believe they would suffer something be afraid, and by
those, of those things, and at that time. Neither those who are in
great good fortune or believe they are believe they would suffer
(therefore they are insolent, contemptuous, and rash, and wealth,
strength, a great number of friends, and power make them of this
sort), nor those who believe they have already suffered every terrible thing and are coldly indifferent to the future, just as those who
have already been tortured on a plank; but there must subsist some
hope of recovery, about which they are in distress. Here is a sign:
Fear makes men capable of deliberation, yet no one deliberates
about the hopeless. Hence one has to put them in that state, whenever it is better for them to be afraid, by saying that they are the sort
to suffer (for even greater people suffered) and to show people of
that sort suffering or having suffered, and by the sort they believed
they would not, and those things which they believed they would
not and at a time when they believed they would not.

1385b11–1386b7:
Let us speak of what sorts of things are pitiable and whom men pity,

and in what state they themselves are. Let pity be a pain for an apparent evil, either destructive or painful, that befalls someone who does not deserve it, which either he too would expect to suffer or would expect one of his own to suffer, and this when it appears near at hand. It is clear that it is necessary that he who is going to pity must be from the start the sort as to believe he would suffer some evil, either himself or one of his own, and the evil be of the sort that has been stated in the definition, either like it or close to it; therefore neither those who are completely devastated pity (for they believe they would no longer suffer anything, for they have suffered), nor those who believe they are super-happy, but rather they are insolent; for if they believe all the goods are theirs, the good that consists in the impossibility of suffering any evil is obviously theirs as well, for this is one of the goods. Those who are of the sort to believe they would suffer are those who have already suffered and have escaped, and the elderly both because of their thoughtfulness and experience, and the weak, and those who are rather cowardly, and the educated; for they able to calculate; and those who have parents or children or wives; for these are one's own and the aforementioned evils are the sort that they can suffer. And those who feel no affect of courage, such as anger or confidence (for these states do not take the future into consideration), nor those in a hubristic disposition (for they too do not consider they will suffer anything), but those who are between these, nor in turn are not very much afraid; for those who have been struck dumb in terror do not pity, because they are involved in their own experience; and if they believe any are good; for he who believes that no one is good will believe that everyone is deserving of evil. And in general whenever one is in a state as to recall the sorts of things that happened to himself or to one of his own, or expects that it happen to himself or one of his own.

Now it has been stated what condition they are in who pity; and it is clear from the definition what things they pity. Everything that is destructive if it is painful is pitiable, and everything annihilating, and as many evils with magnitude of which chance is the cause. Deaths and outrages to the body, ill-usage, old age, illnesses, starvation are painful and destructive, and of evils of which chance is the cause are lack of friends or the fewness of friends (therefore to be torn apart from one's friends and familiars is pitiable), ugliness, weakness, lameness, and the occurrence of some evil to whom it was fitting that there be some good from the start, and the frequent occurrence of these sorts of things, and the occurrence of some good when one has suffered, for example the goods sent from the great king of Persia to Diopeithes when he was already dead, or the fact that no good has happened or there is no possibility of enjoying the goods that did happen.

These things and those like them are what men pity; and they pity acquaintances, if they are not very close to them by ties of kinship (in their case their feelings are as if about their future selves; so the son of Amasis did not burst into tears when his son was being led to his death, as they say, but he did for a friend who was begging,[7] for the latter is pitiable, the former terrible; for the terrible is different from the pitiable and has the capacity to drive out pity, and it is often useful for the contrary; for men no longer pity when the terrible is near to them); and they pity those who are alike in point of age, character, state, rank, and family; for in all these cases it appears that it would more belong to oneself than otherwise; for in general, in this case too one must assume that as many things as men fear for themselves, they pity when they happen to others. Since experiences that appear close at hand are pitiable, what happened ten thousand years ago or will happen ten thousand years in the future, men do not remember in the former case and do not expect in the latter, and so either in general do not pity or not in the same way, it is necessary that those who enhance their

---

[7]   See Herodotus 3.14–15.

performance by gestures,[8] voices, and dress, and in general by their acting be more pitiable (for they make the evil appear near at hand, setting it before one's eyes either as what is about to be or has just been; and events that just happened or are soon to happen are more pitiable). And more pitiable too because of this are the signs: the dress of those who have suffered and everything of the sort, their actions, their speeches, and everything else in which they are engaged while suffering, for example when they are already dying. And especially to be good while involved in events of this sort is pitiable; for all these things increase the pity because they make it appear close by, both because he does not deserve it and the evil appears right in front of one.

1405a34–b3:
And further, one should not make far-fetched metaphors but we should make metaphors from what is akin and of a like sort, and transfer them to the unnamed by way of giving them a name, so that once it is stated it is clear that it is akin, for example in the following well known enigma: "I saw a man welding bronze on a man with fire." For what happened [*pathos*] is nameless, but both involve some kind of attachment. He therefore said the application of the cupping instrument to be a welding.

1410b10–27:
Learning is pleasant for all, and names signify something, so that as many names as make us learn are most pleasant. Now foreign words [*glôttai* – words of another dialect] are unknown, but we know the names in use. Metaphor is especially effective in this regard. Whenever one calls old age stubble, it brings about learning and knowledge through the genus; for both are things that have faded and lost their bloom. Now the similes (images) of poets do the

[8]   The word is *schêmata*.

same; and if they do it well, they are clever and witty; for the simile is, as was said before, a metaphor that has an additional [word],[9] therefore it is less pleasant, for it is longer and does not say, "That's it!" The soul accordingly does not go on a search in that case. It is necessary that those enthymemes be clever that give us swift understanding. Neither superficial enthymemes are well regarded (we mean by superficial what is plain to everyone and whatever do not require any seeking), nor as many as we fail to understand even after they have been spoken, but all those are well regarded either when recognition occurs as soon as they are spoken (even if there were no prior knowledge) or when understanding lags just a little behind. A sort of learning then occurs, but not in the other cases.

1412a11–15:
It has been stated before that one must use metaphors from what is at hand and not obvious, just as in philosophy it is characteristic of the insightful to observe the like even in things that are very far apart, as Archytas did when he said that an arbiter and an altar are the same, for the wronged has recourse to both.

4. Pseudo-Aristotle *Problemata*
920a8–10:
Why is there no choral song in tragedy in the hypodorian or hypophrygian mode? Is it because it has no antistrophe? Rather, it is from the stage, for it is mimetic.[10]

---

9   Compare Longinus, *On the Sublime* 32.3 (=Aristotle fr. 131 Rose):
     "Aristotle and Theophrastus say that these expressions, "as it were," "just
     as if," "if one has to speak in this way," and "if one must speak rather dar-
     ingly," soften bold metaphors; for the plea to be excused, they say, heals
     the venturous phrase.

10   Consider Pseudo-Plutarch, *de musica* 1136D: "Aristoxenus says that
     Sappho was the first to invent the Mixolydian mode, and it was from her

922b10–27:

Why do choruses in tragedy sing neither in the hypodorian nor hypophrygian mode? Is it because these scales least admit of song, which a chorus most needs? The hypophrygian has a practical character; therefore in the *Geryon* [of Nicomachus] the exodus and the arming-scene have been made in it, and the hypodorian has the magnificent and steadfast, and therefore is the scale most adapted to the lyre. Both of these are not suitable for a chorus, but they are more appropriate for those on the stage. For they are imitators of heroes, and the chieftains of the ancients were only heroes; but the peoples (armies) were human beings, of which the chorus is. Accordingly, the mournful and quiet character and song suit it, for they are characteristic of the human. All the other scales have this, but least of all the hypophrygian; for it is enthusiastic and bacchic. We do undergo something in conformity with the mournful scale; and the weak are more susceptible to it than the powerful; accordingly it suits choruses; on the other hand, we act in conformity with the hypodorian and the hypophrygian, which is not proper to a

that the tragic poets learned it; they took it over at any rate and yoked it with the Dorian mode, since the Dorian renders the magnificent and dignified, and the Mixolydian suffering, and through the two of them tragedy has become a mixture," as well as Cleonides' *isagoge harmonica* 13 (p. 206 Jan): "Modulation occurs in the performance of a song whenever the modulation is from an expansive to a contracted or quiet character. The expansive character of a song is that through which magnificence and an elevated manliness of soul are indicated, as well as heroic actions and the experiences proper to heroes. Tragedy employs it most of all and makes use of everything that is connected with this kind. A contracted character is that through which the soul shrinks into humility and an unmanly disposition. A state of this sort fits erotic experiences, lamentations for the dead, expressions of pity and the like. A quiet character of song is that which a quietness of soul, a state of freedom, and peace accompany. Hymns, paeans, praises, counsels and the like suit it."

chorus. For the chorus is a mourner who does not act, for it offers only goodwill to those in its presence.

5. Aristotle *Politics*
1340a14–b17:

Since it happens that music is one of the pleasant things, and virtue is concerned with right enjoyment and in rightly loving and hating, the young must plainly learn and get accustomed to nothing so much as right judgment and enjoyment of sound characters and noble actions. Likenesses of anger and gentleness in rhythms and songs are closest to genuine and true natures, and there are likenesses as well of manliness and moderation and all their opposites, and of all other states and dispositions of character (and this is plain from what we do, for we alter in our soul on hearing things of these sorts); and the getting used to things in their likenesses through pain and joy is close to having the same manner in point of truth. For example, if someone takes pleasure in contemplating an image for no other cause than the shape itself, it is necessary that the contemplation of the thing itself, whose image he contemplates, be pleasant for him. It turns out that in the case of all other perceptible things there is no basis for a likeness for characters, for example in the case of taste and touch, and in the case of sight just barely. (There are shapes of this sort, but they are little effective, and not everyone has a share in this sort of perception; and further they are not likenesses of characters, but rather the shapes and colors that occur are signs of characters, and these in turn are bodily impressions of the passions. It is not that there is not a difference also in the contemplation of these things, and the young must not contemplate the paintings of Pauson, but those of Polygnotus and any other painter or sculptor who depicts character). It is in songs just by themselves that there are imitations of characters. This is obvious. The nature of the scales (harmonies) is right from the start

different, so that listeners are disposed in different ways and do not
maintain the same way in regard to each of them, but to some scales
they are disposed more mournfully and constrainedly, for example,
to the so-called mixolydian, but to others they are disposed more
softly in their thought, for example to the unrestrained and relaxed
scales, and they are disposed in a middle and composed way most in
relation to another scale (of the scales only the Dorian is thought to
do this), and the Phrygian is thought to induce "enthusiasm."
Those who have philosophized about this education speak beautifully, for the witnesses they cite for their arguments are the deeds
themselves. Rhythms too are in the same way. Some have a more
stabilizing character, others stimulate, and of these some admit of
more vulgar motions, others more befitting a free man. It is evident
from this that music is capable of making the character of the soul
be of a certain sort, and if it is capable it is plain that it must be
applied to the young and they be educated in it. Instruction in
music is fitting to a nature of this age; for the young do not willingly
abide anything unpleasant, and music is by nature one of the sweeteners. There is a kinship of resemblance in scales and rhythms to
the soul; accordingly, some of the wise say that the soul is a harmony, and others that it has a harmony.

6. Aristotle *Nicomachean Ethics*
1145a15–33:
After this we must make a new beginning and say that there are
three species of character to be avoided, vice, lack of self-control,
and bestiality. The contraries to two of them are clear; for we call
one of them virtue and the other self-control; but in regard to bestiality it would be most appropriate to say of a virtue that is beyond
us that it is something heroic and divine, just as Homer has made
Priam say of Hector that he was exceedingly good, "He did not
even seem to be the son of a man but rather of a god." Hence, if, as

they say, gods come to be from human beings on account of sur-
passing virtue, it would be clear that the condition set in opposition
to the bestial would be of this sort. For just as there is not even vice
for a beast any more than a virtue, so there is none of a god, but the
latter is more estimable than virtue, and the former a genus somewhat other than vice. Since it is rare that there be a divine man – the
Spartans are accustomed to use this form of address whenever they
admire someone very much (they say, *seios anêr* [divine man]) – so
too the bestial is rare among human beings; but it especially occurs
among barbarians, and some occur on account of illness and impairment; and we give an ill-omened name to those human beings who
are surpassingly vicious.

1148b15–34:
Since some things are pleasant by nature, and of these some are so
without qualification, and others depend on the types of animals
and human beings, and others are not, but some become so on
account of an impairment, others on account of habit, and still others on account of vicious natures, it is possible to observe in each
case corresponding conditions. I am speaking of the bestial conditions, for example, the woman who split open pregnant women and
ate their children, and of the sorts of things they say some of the
savages in the Pontine region enjoy, for some enjoy raw meat and
others human beings, and some lend their children to each another
for the purpose of feasting, or what is reported about Phalaris.
These conditions are bestial, but some arise on account of illnesses
(to some too on account of madness, just as the one who sacrificed
and ate his mother, and he who ate the liver of his fellow-slave), but
other conditions are sickly or from habit, for example the plucking
at the hair or nibbling on fingernails, and further the eating of ash
and earth, and besides these sexual intercourse with males, for
though in some cases it happens by nature, still in others it is from
habit, because they were outraged from childhood. Now in the case

of those where nature is responsible no one would say of them that they lacked self-control, just as one would not say it of women because they do not cover but are covered; and likewise in the case of all who are sickly on account of habit.

Index of Proper Names and Titles[1]

---

[1] An asterisk indicates a doubtful reading; a plus sign indicates that the name occurs more than once in the same context. Only the last two numbers of the Bekker pagination are cited (e.g., 47a rather than 1447a). Line numbers refer to the Greek text; accordingly they may vary as much as several lines in the English translation.

Thyestes: of Carcinus, 54b23
Timotheus: 48a15
*Trojan Women: 59b7
Tydeus: of Theodectes, 55a9

Tyro: of Sophocles, 54b25

Xenarchus: 47b10
Xenophanes: 61a1

Word Index[1]

Account (*logos*): 49a9, 54b18, 55a34, 55b1, 17; *See also* Mean, Say, Speak, and Speech

Act, acting (*prattein*): 48a1, 23, 27, 48b1, 49b31, 37, 50a6, 21, 50b4, 52a36, 55a25, 59a15, 59b24; *see also* Do (*prattein*) 51a32, 51b11

Action, acting (*praxis, praktikon*): 47a28, 48b25, 49b24, 36, 50a1, 2, 4, 16, 18, 50b3, 24, 51a18, 19, 28, 31, 51b29, 33, 52a2, 13, 14, 37, 53b16, 27, 54a18, 59a19, 22, 59b1, 60a1, 62b11; *see also* Being in action

Ambiguity, ambiguous (*amphibolia, amphibolon*): 61a25, 26

Analogy (*analogon*): 48b38, 57b9, 16, 57b25

Anapest (*anapaistos*): 52b24

Anger, angry (*orgê, orgizesthai*): 55a32, 56b1; *see also* irrascible

Animal (*zôion*): 48b7, 50b34, 38, 51a3, 4, 59a20

Architectonic (*architektonikê*): 56b11

Art (*technê*): 47a20, 21, 47b29, 50b20, 51a7, 24, 53a22, 54a10, 60b15, 19, 23, 28, 30, 61b24, 62a1, 62b12

Artless, less artful, least artful (*atechnos*): 50b17, 53b8, 54b20, 28, 31

Astounding (*ekplêktikos, ekplêxis*): 54a4, 55a17, 60b25

August (*semnos*): 48b25, 58a21

Bad, badly (*kakos, kakôs*): 56a10, 18, 61a12; *see also* Evil, Vice, Worse, and Wretchedness

Barbarism (*barbarismos*): 58a24

---

[1]   We have not differentiated the occurrences of words clustered under a single heading—e.g., "tragedy" and "tragic"—and have not indicated multiple occurences on a single line. Only the last two numbers of the Bekker pagination are cited (e.g., 47a rather than 1447a). Line numbers refer to the Greek text; accordingly they may vary by as much as several lines in the English translation. The cluster of Greek words following each entry in parentheses correspond collectively but not necessarily individually to the cluster of English words constituting the entry.